Julia Anna Wolcott

Song-Blossoms

Julia Anna Wolcott

Song-Blossoms

ISBN/EAN: 9783744651677

Printed in Europe, USA, Canada, Australia, Japan

Cover: Foto ©Thomas Meinert / pixelio.de

More available books at **www.hansebooks.com**

SONG-BLOSSOMS

BY

JULIA ANNA WOLCOTT.

I found the poems in the fields,
And only wrote them down.
　　　　　JOHN CLARE, of Northampton.

BOSTON.
ARENA PUBLISHING CO.,
COPLEY SQUARE,
1895.

60201

Copyrighted by
JULIA ANNA WOLCOTT
1894.
All Rights Reserved.

Dedicated

MOST TENDERLY, REVERENTLY,
AND WITH PROFOUNDEST GRATITUDE,
TO THE MEMORY OF
MY MOTHER,

ANNA EAMES WOLCOTT.

I thought this little book to place
Within thy warm, enfolding hand,—
To watch the pleasure light thy face
As sunshine lighteth up the land.

NOTE.—Special thanks, for permission to use certain copyrighted poems, are returned to the publishers of the *Arena Magazine, Century Magazine, New England Magazine, Congregationalist, Well-Spring, Illustrated Christian Weekly, Ladies' Home Journal,* and to the former and present publishers of *Little Men and Women*—the Lothrop Publishing Co., and the Alpha Publishing Co.

TABLE OF CONTENTS.

RIVERSIDE AND MEADOW.

Joy Doubled	11
Where	12
In the Meadows in June	14
The Quest	18
The Wild Gerardia	20
By the Brook	22
The Bee	24
The Spring Pasture	26
Autumn's Coming	28
Milkweed-down	29
Spiranthes	31

AMONG THE HILLS.

Aurora's Coming	37
On the Hills	39
Invocation to the Hills	43
The Useless Little Tree	44

BY THE WAYSIDE.

Daisies and Succory	53
The Yellowbird	55
The Mayweed	57

HERE AND THERE.

Regret	61
Dependence	62
Sunset on the Bay	63
Loch Katrine	65
Hold Fast the Bright Hours	69
Call to the Crocuses	70
A Breath	72
Valentine Song	74
Dream of Schooldays	78

AT THE FIRESIDE.

Coming Home at Night	85
To Woman Who Toileth	87
The Land Where We All Have Been	90
The Cradle in which John Quincy Adams was Rocked	93
The Children's Saint	97

WITH THE CHILDREN.

Santa Claus's Sister	103
Wedding in the Garden	107
Lady Marie's Mishap	111
Giving	114
If I were a Boy instead of a Girl	117
The Prisoner of the Snow Fort	120
Kitty's Birthday Party	122
Birthday Letter to Flossie	124
The Child and the Aster	128
My Little Milkmaid	133
How They Started for the Fair	135

Helping Zeke 137
Bessie's Riches 143
The May Party 146
Arbor-day Song 154

IN LIGHTSOME MOOD.

Our Christmas 157
The Mugwump 161
The Jealous Ghost 163
Andrea's Discovery 170
The Usurer's Reply 173
Advice to a Despairing Lover 175
When Pushed to the Wall 176

GREETINGS.

An Old, Old Fashioned Flower 179
November Greeting 181
Greeting with Bluebells 183
Chime for a September Wedding 184
Welcome to Baby 186

TRANSLATIONS.

The Mountain Emigrant 189
Carcassonne 192
The Ploughman and his Children 196
Child-times 197
The Castle by the Sea 200

IN THE SANCTUARY.

Easter Lilies	205
The Broader Field	207
The Woodbird's Song	209
She Is Not Dead	215
Joy and Pain	218
Invalided	220
Up or Down	222
Her First Sunday in Heaven	225
Come Back	227
At the Tomb of Dickens	229
In Chains	231
The Burial of a Master	234
Departure of the Old Year	239
The Old and the New	241
Two Prayers	245
Birthday Hymn	246
Hymn for Help	247
Lend a Hand	248
Sunset Hymn	250
Benediction	252

RIVERSIDE AND MEADOW.

Joy Doubled.

I SING as sings the bird
  On yonder branchlet swinging;
It is not that the song be heard,
  But for the joy of singing.
    And yet, if there chance by,
    Or hap to linger nigh,
Who listens to my lay,
  Then, with a heart less troubled,
Goes braver forth to meet the day,—
  The joy of song is doubled.

Where?

Oh where does the blush of the wild-rose go,
    When it fades from the bank of the stream?
And tell me, dearest, if you know,
    What becomes of the marigold's gleam?

Oh where is the little blue succory flower,
    That drooped beside the way?
And where the joy only born for an hour,
    And the hope that lived but a day?

Are the sweets all lost of the flower that dies,
    Ere the honey-bee comes to sip?
And wasted the breath of the lover's sighs
    That fall unheard from the lip?

Oh where is the lay that the bobolink trilled
    When summer was young and gay?
Is the sweet song ringing yet unstilled,
    Floating through space away?

The rose's blush that fades by the stream
    To the sunset lends its dye;
The gay marsh-marigolds glow and gleam,
    The stars of the midnight sky.

The little blue succory blooms again,
    In the eyes of the girl I love;
And I think all the hopes and joys that wane
    Await our coming above.

The flower that dies ere the honey-bee sips
    Gives its sweets to the winds that roam;
The sighs, unheard as they fall from the lips,
    Waft love's fond messages home.

And the melody gay of the bobolink's song,
    Though it falls no more on our ears,
Is mingling yet, as it drifts along,
    With the music of the spheres.

In the Meadows in June.

Oh the blue, blue sky is o'er me,
   The grass waves round my feet;
The river rolls before me,
   The robin's note is sweet.

Their streamers the flags are flying,
   The buttercups gleam like gold;
The breeze with joy is sighing,
   The regal ferns unfold.

The clematis stars grow whiter,
   The elder has blossoms of snow;
And the fairy lilies are brighter
   Than flowers of the garden know.

Oh the budding rose, with lips parted,
    And the far and feathery rue,
And the daisies, golden-hearted,
    And the clovers wet with dew,

With the grasses bend and shimmer,
    When the wind comes rippling down,
Till the meadow's all a'glimmer,
    Like my Lady's broidered gown.

And the breezes, swaying and lifting
    The billows of shining bloom,
Set a myriad wavelets drifting,
    Of a mingled, rich perfume.

And many an unseen flower,
    I know by its odor sweet,
Is hidden in yonder bower,
    Or blooms about my feet.

And to think that these marvels of sweetness,—
    By the kiss of the dew and the sun,—
In their color and form and completeness,
    From the brown old earth were won!

Oh miracles!—never ending
    In this glorious world of ours!
There's no greater, to me, than the sending
    Of the beauty and wealth of flowers.

Not even the constellation,
    Which gleams from the midnight sky,
Is more wondrous than the creation
    Of these flower-stars 'neath my eye.

Oh the riches that God is giving,
    In color and fragrance and tune!
Oh the rapturous joy of living,
    That is felt in the meadows in June!

It is seen in the happy quiver
    Of a thousand bright-hued wings;
It is heard in the chant that the river,
    In its grateful gladness brings.

It is shown in the dance and flutter
    Of a million blossoming things;
And oh, that my lips might utter
    The song that my spirit sings!

Oh I 'd live in the meadows forever!
    And I 'd have all the days like this!
Then joy would vanish never,
    And only to be, were bliss!

The Quest.

Namesake of the sweet cuckoo,
Buttercups, and daisies too,
Violets with your eyes of blue,
Clovers fair or rose in hue!
Tell me quick, and tell me true!
Has my Love been seen by you?
Did she pass the meadow through?

Little clouds that sail on high,
Swallows flitting through the sky,
Winds that pass me with a sigh,
Have you seen my Love go by?
Strays she far, or is she nigh? —
Naught will pause or make reply.
If I find her not I die!

Caught the flutter of her dress?
Primrose, primrose, tell and bless!
Did her feet this pathway press?
And these ferns her hand caress?
Primrose, mocking my distress,
Shakes her head and bids me guess;
But the trillium 's nodding Yes.

The Wild Gerardia.

Through mazes bright of August bloom
  I careless ran, one shining day,
Nor paused to pluck the primrose tall,
  Or golden-rod that lit the way.

But when, beneath my very feet,
  A frail gerardia blushing grew,—
O'ershadowed by the lofty blooms,
  Its modest flowers of sunset hue,—

I stooped with joy my prize to gain,
  With eager haste I snapped the stem,
And held the dainty thing aloft,
  To mark each little rosy gem.

But while I, raptured, gazed upon
    My new possession, fresh and fair,
And watched with glee the tiny bells
    All quivering in the scented air,

And cried exultant: "It is mine!
    Mine, wholly mine, its beauty bright,
I'll wear it all this golden day
    Upon my breast with proud delight!"

They lost their slender, trembling hold,
    And from my sight fell, one by one;
Within my hand the naked stem
    Was outlined dark against the sun.

By the Brook.

By the brook that laughs and plays,
When the robin sang his lays,
And the wild-rose blushed as brightly as the morn,
There two youthful lovers strayed,
And her hand in his was laid,
And their hearts, it seemed, for joy alone were born.

Now have come the wintry days,
And no birds with roundelays
Greet the coming of the sad and wintry morn;
Not a wild-rose glads the glade,
Streams are dumb, and rush and blade
In the wind are shivering lifeless and forlorn.

By the brook the youth still strays,
    Sad and listless are his ways,
For the rose of joy from out his heart is torn;
    All his part in life is played,
    And of death he's not afraid,
Since the maiden that he loved from earth is borne.

Once again with roundelays
    Glad birds greet the summer days,
And the wild-rose blushes brightly as the morn;
    Through the green and leafy glade
    Murmurs steal, by waters made,
Branch and vine with blossoms everywhere adorn.

By the brook the youth still strays,
    Bright his eye, alert his ways,
All forgotten are the wintry days forlorn;
    By his side another maid,—
    In his hand her hand is laid;
In his heart the rose of joy again is born.

The Bee.

I watched the cloud-rack sweep the sky,
I felt the storm that hovered nigh,
And heard the sad-voiced winds go by.

The skies that arched my soul grew dark,
And, dull with gloom, I did not hark
To song of bird, or beauty mark.

The aster-plumes waved round my way,
The golden-rod was nodding gay
To butterflies in bright array.

Among the flowers there came a bee;
A merry, bustling fellow, he,
Who sang his song right merrily.

He cared not though the skies were gray;
His little heart was just as gay;
He gathered honey all the way.

With lighter heart I watched the bee,
And cried: "I'm surely brave as he!
The storm shall bring no gloom to me!"

The Spring Pasture.

Oh, oft in my dreams I am wandering still
Through the pleasant Spring Pasture, beside the
    bright rill;
There I visit each haunt that in childhood I knew,
And gather the gentians with fringes of blue.

I pluck the wild-roses that lean o'er the stream,
And drink in their fragrance again in my dream;
While the elder's fair blossoms, and cornel's pure
    snow,
Reflected I see in the wavelets below.

I search for wild strawberries! —Were real ones as
    sweet?—
And braid the long grasses that grow at my feet;
Count the threads in the web that the brook spider
    weaves,
And pull the sweet-flag with its ribbon-like leaves,

The spring's fragile beauties, the midsummer's pride,
And the late autumn blossoms I find side by side;
For in Dreamland all seasons are mingled in one,
There 's no day without flowers, no hour without sun.

So my apron 's o'erflowing with asters and rue,
And snowdrops and cowslips and violets too ;
And jack-in-the-pulpit peeps out at the end,
And their sweets the azaleas and columbines blend;

While the cardinal's blossoms and loosestrife's bright gold,
Again my small fingers with rapture enfold.
Oh, blessed it is, when our youth is all o'er,
That the joys of our childhood in dreams come once more !

Autumn's Coming.

Autumn's coming! Even now
Bends the heavy orchard bough;
And the apples first to mellow,
Globes of russet, ruby, yellow,
   Gem the fading grass.
And this morning I have found,
On the low, spring-watered ground,
Just unfolding, the first gentian;
And the crickets hold convention
   Nightly, where I pass.

Yet I mourn not, breathe no sigh,
When the blossoms round me die:
For as, in their rich completeness,
Hold the fruits the sun and sweetness
   Of the summer o'er,
So the beauty that is past,
Robins' songs, and rose-leaves cast,
Perfumes, wave on wave that drifted,
Sun-gold, through the leaf-roofs sifted,
   In my heart I store.

Milkweed-Down.

A CHILD from the folds of his tiny gown
Had plucked a bit of the milkweed's down,
One autumn day, in the meadow brown.

As its silken threads in the air blew free,
In wonder and glee he laughed to see
A feather of silver filigree.

And he loosed the grasp of his soft, pink hand,
And he watched it float, this shining strand,
And rise and fall, by the light air fanned.

Then he longed to see it soar up on high;
Though it felt but the power of his baby sigh,
It sailed away, through the bright blue sky.

And in vain the child, in the meadow brown,
Reached his dimpled hands for that bit of down,
And cried, in his grief, "Come down! come down!"

Oh dear little man, of the meadow brown,
Who wept in vain for the milkweed-down,
There 's many a one, in grown-up-town,

Who has thrust some treasure as lightly aside;
Then, vainly, while striving his grief to hide,
Has sought it sadly, both far and wide.

Spiranthes.

When the autumn days are here,
When the meadow 's brown and sere,
    When the primrose gold is wasted,
    And the clover's sweets all tasted,
And the frost-king hovers near;

When the cardinal, fiery red,
Passion-wearied, droops his head;
    When the loosestrife 's lived her hour,
    And the cranesbill's purple flower,
With the dust of earth is wed;

When the scent of violet bloom,
And the clethra's sweet perfume,
    That, like ghosts of blossoms fair,
    Haunted all the summer air,
Linger not in autumn gloom;

When the wild brier's wrinkled hip
Shows where glowed the rose's lip,—
    As the withered cheek of crone
    Tells where maiden blushes shone,—
And the bee finds naught to sip;

When the tender onoclea
Shivers in the wind from fear;
    When the grape-fern casts her fruit,
    And the rue, in changèd suit,
Mourns above the summer's bier;

In a nook, all fair and sweet,
Where the south slope juts to greet
    Willows twined in thickest hedge ;
    Where the blue-eyed grass and sedge
Lightly kiss the passing feet ;

Watered by a little rill,
Sheltered from the winds that chill,
    Where the lady-fern is seen
    Latest in her dress of green,
Just where meadow meets with hill ;

There the pure spiranthes blow,
And, from out their lips of snow,
    Breath of fragrance, passing sweet,
    Subtly fills the lone retreat,
Till no loss the meadows know.

So, perchance, 't will be, some day,
When life's summer 's sped away,
    With its glow of pride and passion,
    With its blossoms joy can fashion,
And its tumults fierce or gay;

From the ashes of the fires
Of its manifold desires,
    When all longings vain shall cease,
    Will spring forth the root of peace;
—Life springs oft from funeral pyres!

In the heart's calm autumn hour
'T will put forth its pure white flower;
    As its petals fair unroll,
    Fragrance sweet will fill the soul
With content, her richest dower.

AMONG THE HILLS.

Aurora's Coming.

Oh fair is the morning!
The blossoms, adorning
Meadow and mountain,
Are wet from the fountain
Whence Nature distributes
The dew that contributes
Its share of bright gems to Aurora's fair crown.
The sun all his lances
Sends out as warm glances,
To woo the fair maiden
Approaching us laden,
Through the sky's eastern portals,
With rich gifts for mortals
Of light and of color, that stream from her gown.

There 's a stir, a commotion,
O'er land and o'er ocean;
'T is the heart of creation
In glad palpitation;
All nature is voicing
Its thrill of rejoicing! —
Throughout the long darkness with sadness 't was dumb.
Every bird that is winging
The ether, is singing
A song of thanksgiving! —
Oh rapture of living!
For with light has come sweetness,
Triumphant completeness!
Aurora, the queen of the morning, has come!

On the Hills.

Pray what do you see, with your great brown eyes,
Oh golden-robed daisies, high up on the hills?
Do you watch the clouds float through the soft summer skies?
Do you see the green meadows and sparkling rills?

Do you look for the sun in the east every morn,
And mark his descent in the west each eve?
Are you glad when the day, like a rose, is born?
When it lies in its shroud of night, do you grieve?

When the storm-cloud bursts, with a crash, o'erhead,
  And the lightning darts to the crag that is near;
When the tall pine falls to the earth, torn and dead,
  Do you tremble with awe? Are you pale with fear?

When the rainbow its arch rears over your hills,
  Do you hail its bright hues with a throb of delight?
Know you aught of the promise its coming fulfils?
  Has a little bird sung it to you in her flight?

I know you 're contented, light-hearted, and gay;
  For you dance with your neighbor, the blossoming grass;
And you court'sy and nod, in the blithest way,
  To each zephyr, sweet-laden, that chances to pass;

Yet, look you not down on the dwellings of men,
  And dream of the worlds that their dumb walls enfold? —
Like us, ponder on what is beyond your ken?
  Is there nothing in common with mortals you hold?

Ah well, golden daisies, you 're happy, you 're blest,
  Whatever your dreams, in a home on the hills;
For naught comes to your life but of peace and of rest;
  You 're above the poor world, with its frets and its ills.

You 're so near the blue sky you seem close up to God;
  His stars watch you solemnly all the calm night;
While the sunshine by day falls free on the sod.
  Ah me, were a home on the hills my right, —

Where the winds, unfettered, sweep grandly along,
  Fraught with the balm of the fir-tree and pine;
Where the ear is caressed by the hill-brook's song,
  And the air gives life like a rich, strong wine!

The eye from horizon to zenith may roam,
  For no walls, reared by man, their barriers impose;
All is free as the torrents that leap and that foam,
  For a home on the hills where the gold daisy glows!

Ah well, though no height-crowning mansion I own,
  Each soul has a palace wherever it wills;
I will strive to climb up, by the best I have known,
  Till my spirit dwells tranquil and free on life's hills.

Invocation to the Hills.

Give me of your strength and grandeur,
    Hills, oh everlasting hills! —
Of the joy forever pulsing
    In the rhythm of your rills, —
Of the patient calm endurance
    That is conquered by no ills.

Strong you 've stood, from feet vale-planted,
    To your fragrant, dark pine locks,
Meeting storms and wild tornadoes
    With the breastplate of your rocks.
Give me breastplate of your courage
    To withstand life's rudest shocks.

From your sides the torrents rushing
    Carry wealth to vales below;
Teach pure springs of love and mercy
    Ceaseless from my heart to flow, —
That I give to souls about me,
    That I lessen human woe!

The Useless Little Tree.

In an earth-filled cleft of a rocky-steep,
    High up on a wind-swept hill,
A little seed sprang up one day,
    And it flourished by God's will.

And year by year, through sun and shower,
    It grew till a brave young tree,
Against the rough and barren ledge,
    The traveller might see.

And though by wind and jutting rock
    Of its symmetry bereft,
Its gnarlèd roots like bands of iron
    Lay bedded in the cleft.

And firmly they held the little tree
  That grew so near the sky,
Though the gale that swept its leafy head
  Blew never so fierce and high.

But it often sighed, and wearily said,—
  As it looked on the vale below,
And watched the trees in their sheltered home
  In grace and majesty grow,—

" Oh why must I stand on this barren rock
  With hardly a hold for my feet,
To be tossed and torn by every wind
  And pierced by the driving sleet?

" On my stunted limbs no fruit is hung
  To cool and refresh mankind;
And 'neath my branches, when summer is hot,
  No shade does the traveller find;

"While never a bird to my wind-swept boughs
   Comes its nest to build or to sing !
Alas ! I am doomed to live and die,
   A poor and useless thing."

  .   .   .   .

One morning bright, when the glad green earth
   Seemed fresh from the hand of God,
When buds and blossoms were springing forth
   From the warm and pungent sod,

And the honey bee had come out on his quest,—
   For the gracious hand of May
Had scattered the gay little columbines
   All over the ledges gray,—

From flower to flower, with eager step,
   A fair child lightly sprang;
And he plucked the heads of scarlet and gold
   While gaily his sweet voice rang :

"Mamma! dear mamma! do n't stay down there,
　　There is nothing but green below;
Oh come up here and we 'll play on the rocks,
　　Where the beautiful blossoms grow.

"This great gray ledge shall be our house;
　　That rock with a back your seat;
And I 'll plant the pretty columbines
　　For a garden at your feet."

Then quickly the youthful mother sprang,
　　Her face and step like a girl's,
To obey the will of her little king —
　　Her king with his crown of curls.

And lightly she climbed to the rocky height,
　　And she sat on the rude stone seat;
And her little king of the blossoms bright
　　Made a garden about her feet.

And a flowery crown she deftly wove,
   And placed on his shining hair;
And proudly she thought that no ruler before
   Had looked so brave and fair.

And so the moments quickly sped,
   As the golden moments will,
Till there rose on the air a piercing cry,
   And the mother's heart stood still.

"My boy! my boy!" she madly cried,
   And wildly she sprang to clasp
The little form that even then
   Had slipped beyond her grasp.

Alas! too near the shelving edge
   The dancing feet had strayed.
No voice of warning had sounded forth,
   No hand their steps had stayed.

"Oh God!" she gasped, "be merciful!"
  Her lips could frame no more;
Her trembling limbs with terror smote
  Beneath the weight they bore.

Yet on she pressed, now swift and strong,
  To scan the rocks below;
Now faltering, weak and blind with fear,
  Not daring the truth to know.

So came she to the ledge's brink:
  Oh Father, could it be?
Held fast within the circling arm
  Of the little, useless tree,

Unharmed by bruise, unblanched by fear,
  Her boy! her precious child!
He reached his hands up to her own;
  He cried "Mamma!" and smiled.

With arms made strong by love and joy
   She drew him to her breast,
And thick on his rosy cheek and lip
   Her fondest kisses pressed.

"My God, I thank thee!" she weeping cried,
   "Thou hast heard a mother's prayer;
Oh make him worthy of thy great love,—
   Me worthy of my care!"

And then,—and joyous were now the tones
   That late with grief were wild,—
"Oh bless and spare the little tree
   That has saved my darling child!"

Ah! then did the little tree rejoice;
   And it waved each leafy hand;
And it would not have changed its wind-swept
      rock
   For the sunniest vale in the land!

BY THE WAYSIDE.

Daisies and Succory.

"Daisies that faint in the noonday sun,
Succory blossoms, one by one
Closing your eyes of heaven's own blue,
Are you not sorry, I wonder, that you
Came to this dusty road to stay?"
I asked the flowers as I paused by the way.

And they answered with voices never heard,
Save by the bee and the hummingbird,
And the child of man who loves them so well
That he lists for the secrets they have to tell:
"Nay, we would choose this place to live,
For here by the way we may always give.

"Only this morn came a young girl by,
With heavy burden and weary eye,
Who stopped to rest by our side awhile;
Then she went her way with a radiant smile.
And a baby, chubby, and good to see,
Kissed our faces with cries of glee.

"Then a man who is worldly and proud and cold
Forgot his ambition,—forgot his gold;
And with softened face, and a starting tear,
Gathered some blossoms, kneeling here,
To carry to one who may never go
Where the grasses wave, and the wildflowers
    blow."

The Yellowbird.

There 's a gay little yellowbird flitting about
   In the maple just over the way,
'Mong the scarlet twigs, now in and now out,
Now pausing, as if some wish or doubt
   Had bidden his wings delay.

Oh dear little bird, with your golden vest,
   I hope you 'll decide to stay;
For nothing shall ever your brood molest,
If you 'll come and build your beautiful nest
   Of lichens all green and gray.

I can see Mrs. Yellowbird down by the spring;
   Go sing her each word that I say;
And, while she is preening her breast and her wing,
I'm sure you'll have time to decide everything:
   Then come and select your spray.

And on darksome days, how pleasant 't will seem,
   When the sun has gone away,
And forgotten to leave a single beam,
To see your bright forms through the branches
   gleam,
   As you flutter and dart in your play.

Oh, the winds of summer shall softly blow,
   And gently your nest shall sway;
And the whispering leaves shall murmur low
A lullaby sweet that the maple-trees know:
   O Yellowbird, do not say nay!

The Mayweed.

I AM naught but a little mayweed,
   By the dusty road I grow;
And the people who pass o'erlook me,
   I am so small and low.

But God in his might and glory,
   High up in the heavens so blue,
He sees the little mayweed,
   And gives it both sun and dew.

So, child, whom the dear Lord's wisdom
   Has placed in a humble cot,—
Toiling in common raiment,
   O'erlooked in your weary lot,—

Grieve not, though men pass by you!
  God sees you, and knows your load,—
As He sees the little mayweed,
  That grows by the dusty road.

HERE AND THERE.

Regret.

Wouldst dim this shining day
Because one, passed for aye,
Was hung with clouds of gray?
Nay, fling regret away!
Be strong in joy to-day;
And bid its living ray
Close in thy brave heart stay,
To light thee on thy way,
Should skies again be gray.

Dependence.

Though grand and unending the rhythm ascending,
From numberless waves, as they roll to the shore,
And deep, awe-compelling, the organ-tones swelling
Wherever, rock-prisoned, the wild breakers roar;
Should the ripples' soft treble among the beach pebble
For a moment be hushed, the sea's anthem were o'er.

Sunset on the Bay.

The wind's asleep, there's not a breath
    To stir the waves to motion ;
The wingèd boats, like birds in death,
    Lie on the breast of ocean.

The lone gull, floating dreamlike by,
    Lifts not his shining pinion ;
No stir or sound, in sea or sky,
    To mar sweet calm's dominion.

The sunset clouds scarce change their shape,
    On the horizon lying,
Though in their light, sail, bay, and cape
    Are brightening — fading — dying.

High on the cliff the tall church-spire
   Points with a gleaming finger;
The lighthouse grim is crowned with fire;
   Oh sunset glory, linger!

E'en yon stern rocks, beneath your kiss,
   Glow as with sweet emotion;
Oh teach my soul the tranquil bliss
   That wraps the sky and ocean!

Loch Katrine.

Musing I glide o'er Katrine's Lake;
I idly mark the foamy wake,
And watch the silvery ripples break
    On Ellen's verdant Isle.

The sun rides high, the waves are bright;
I see the gaily flashing light
Chasing the shadows out of sight,
    Along the leafy shore.

Far o'er the little boat I lean;
I drink the beauty of the scene,
And dream of all that here has been,
    While truth and fiction blend.

And as I gaze the past returns;
Among the hazel and the ferns,
And sunlit bloom that brightly burns,
    Fair Ellen stands revealed.

Within her eye a soft light glows;
Upon her cheek still blooms the rose,
As bright as eglantine that blows
    Upon this rocky isle.

Graceful she stands, of maiden mien,
Yet queenly, from the ringlet's sheen
Down to the arching foot, half seen,—
    True Lady of the Lake!

Rising and falling on the bay,
The wavelets round its sides at play,
I see her shallop as it lay
    When Snowdoun's knight had crossed.

And there, half hidden and half seen,
Within the feathery willow's screen,
Fitz-James himself, in Lincoln green,
   With dripping hounds beside.

And see! through birch and oak spread wide,
The clematis, like froth on tide,
That Ellen's hand has trained to hide
   The rude hall where she dwells.

And mingled with the heron's cry,
And caw of rooks that wing the sky,
And cooling plash of ducks that ply
   The blue and mirroring wave,

So sweet a strain floats on my ear
The ripples hush their rhymes to hear;
The startled hare forgets her fear;
   For wakes the minstrel's harp.

Oh Wizard of the North! the spell
Your magic pen has wrought, to dwell
O'er this fair lake, isle, mount, and dell,
    Shall hold while time shall last.

Till bluebells shall forget to blow,
And purple heather cease to grow,
And Katrine's waves no longer glow
    Beneath the sun's bright glance,

Who comes a pilgrim to this shore
Shall see again the forms of yore,
In fairy boat, with noiseless oar,
    Glide on Loch Katrine's breast.

And form and boat and oar shall sway
With rhythmic motion, to the lay
That Allan-bane, the minstrel gray,
    Still sings with cadence sweet.

Hold Fast the Bright Hours.

Oh let us not cling, with vain sorrowing,
   To the sadness and pain of life!
No blessing will spring from remembering
   Misfortunes or days of strife.

As the bee lays up sweets from the lilies he meets,
   And hurries the wormwood by,
We will hoard the gold that the happy days hold,—
   Let the thought of the bitter ones die.

And no idle regret for the sorrows we 've met
   Shall lessen the joy of to-day;
We 'll hold fast the bright hours, and we 'll gather
     the flowers,
   As we journey along life's way.

A Call to the Crocuses.

The bluebird is calling, the spring rain is falling;
  Awake! little crocuses, leave your dark bed!
The soft winds are blowing, the glad brooks are
    flowing,
  The willow-twigs glisten, all yellow and red.

Oh be not faint-hearted! Old Winter's departed!
  Stay not in your prison of dreary brown mould.
Not a flake of snow lingers! Stretch out your green
    fingers,
  Then lift up your faces of purple and gold.

The robin's note's ringing; the frogs too are singing
  Their low, pleasant music, down by the old mill;
The winds are all bringing, from buds that are
    springing,
  Fresh odors from meadow and wayside and hill.

Oh come from your hiding, nor wait for more
    chiding;
  Lo, now the sun's shining! — there's nothing
    to fear.
Come forth! 'tis your duty! Praise God with your
    beauty —
  The God who gives springtime, and all the round
    year!

A Breath.

Two lovers stood in the twilight dim.
Her dovelike eyes were raised to him;
His face was turned toward the day's gold rim.

The lingering fire in the darkling sky
Lent an added warmth to his speech and eye.
He pled for her love as, when death has come
    nigh,

The desolate pray for a sign from the dead.
Like a flower on its stem, her fair young head
Had drooped at the words, " Shall we not wed?"

Though her heart from her breast, as bird from its
    nest,
At the call of its mate had flown, he guessed
No word of the truth, nor knew he was blessed.

For the pride of a maiden was still her own;
And she paused at the door of the life unknown,
With question, with awe. Though the lovelight
    shone

In her sweet dark eyes, ere she said yea or nay,
The strange new way that before her lay
She must plainer see; she would fain delay.

And she stood, all doubtful, perplexed, and weak;
When a single breath, unfelt on his cheek,
Swift ended the strife, with "Why did you speak?"

Though love's soft ray in her eye still lay,
Her face was turned from the fading day;
And he saw it not, and he went his way.

Valentine Song.

He.

Oh lady fair, thine ear incline;
I bring thee a song for thy valentine.
I sing of thy face, that is fairer than day,
When the sun, like thy smile, chases shadows away,
And thy grace, which inspires this lay of mine.
Wilt thou take my song for thy valentine?
Oh, take it, love, for thy valentine!

She.

Sweet does the melody fall on my ear,
As the bird's first trill when the dawn is near;
And a charm to the lay thy praise has lent;
But a song, when sung, is but breath that is spent.

So, oh minstrel lover mine,
I'll take no song for my valentine!
No, I'll take no song for my valentine!

He.

I bring thee flowers I have culled with care;
Each rose is fit for a queen to wear;
Yet no blossom here, in its beauty and grace,
Is half so fair as thine own sweet face.
I have tied them all in a nosegay fine,
And I bring them to thee for a valentine,—
Oh take them, love, for thy valentine!

She.

Fragrant thy flowers, and fair to see;
I thank thee for gathering them all for me;
But naught care I for bud or flower,
For the fairest blossom fades in an hour;
So the sweetest blooms, from the choicest vine,
Would never do for my valentine,—
No, they never would do for my valentine!

He.

    Oh lady, fair and proud and cold,
    Forgive, forgive, if I make too bold.
    Thou hast spurned my song, and my nosegay sweet;
    Now humbly I cast myself at thy feet;
    And my heart, that o'erflows with love, shall be thine,
    If thou 'lt take it, dear, for thy valentine.—
    Oh take it, dear, for thy valentine!

She.

    Yes, a heart that is warm and true like thine,
    That will I have for my valentine;
    And when songs are hushed, and blossoms depart,
    I still shall be cheered by thy faithful heart;
    And if, in return, thou 'lt care for mine,
    Why, take it, love, for thy valentine,—
    Oh take it, love, for thy valentine!

Together.

Oh a song, when sung, is but breath that is spent,
So a song for a valentine ne'er would content;
And naught care I for bud or flower,
For the fairest blossom fades in an hour;
So the sweetest blooms, from the choicest vine,
Would never do for my valentine,—
Oh they never would do for my valentine!

But a heart that is warm and true like thine,
That will I have for my valentine;
And when songs are hushed, and blossoms depart,
I still shall be cheered by a faithful heart.
And if, in return, thou 'lt care for mine,
Why take it, love, for thy valentine,—
Oh take it, love, for thy valentine!

Dream of Schooldays.

When the god of sleep had touched me,
  With his poppy-wreathèd wand,
And in dreams I floated swiftly,
  All my waking cares beyond,

Lo! you came and stood beside me,
  With the face I loved of old, —
Eyes of azure, calm and tender,
  And the hair of shadowy gold;

And you sat down close beside me,
  And you laid your hand in mine;
And our fingers twined together,
  Like the tendrils of the vine.

Joyous, joyous was the meeting,
   For the parting had been sad;
Sad farewell and weary waiting
   Make the greeting doubly glad.

And your clasp was warm and tender,
   Though no word the silence broke;
Eye and hand have still a language,
   Fraught with meaning lip ne'er spoke.

Talked we then of years departed;
   And with memory wandered back
To the day you left our school-home,
   By the green-fringed Merrimac,—

Left our sea-washed Massachusetts,—
   Classmates, friends, and all the rest,—
For the old home of your childhood,
   In that fair State of the West,

Where the Father of the Waters
  In a little lake is born,
And the sunshine and the shadows
  Fall on wheat and tasseled corn.

And then everything seemed changing,—
  As things do in dreams, you know;
'T was our room at school returning,
  Just as 't was long years ago.

And the laugh of care-free maidens
  Floated through the study door, —
Came the hum of many voices,
  Footsteps on the long hall floor.

And you read those dear old ballads,
  You have read to me so oft;
And your voice was low and tender,
  And your tones were sweet and soft,

Till the rhythm seemed the murmur
    Of a smoothly flowing stream,
And a thousand girlish fancies
    Mingled in the pleasant dream.

But, while I was joyous floating
    On the waves of memory's tide,
From my own your hand kept slipping,
    Till you drifted from my side.

First I could not touch your garments;
    Then the distance grew apace,
Till your golden hair shone misty,
    And I could not see your face.

Then I woke — and, waking, called you,
    By the old, endearing name;
Naught but melancholy echoes
    Through the chilly darkness came;

But the dream has spanned the chasms
   'Twixt the cities Now and Then;
So at will I cross the bridges,
   And I walk with you again, —

Walk with you in fields Elysian,
   Where our school-girl feet once strayed,
When we thought the world made for us,
   And our futures what we prayed;

And the present seems the brighter,
   For the past that looks divine;
And your face I see the plainer,
   Since the vision that was mine.

AT THE FIRESIDE.

Coming Home at Night.

Though dark is the night, and the rough way long,
I hum, as I trudge, an old love-song.
No gloom 's in my heart, in my frame no shiver,
Though a chill comes creeping across the river;
For well I know, when this steep is gained,
Though the stars be few, and the moon has waned,

A light on my path will surely be!
It will stream from the lamp my Rose, for me,
Has trimmed, and placed on the window-sill
Of our dear little cot, just over the hill.
Each night, as I plod through the darkness drear,
It sends me its message of love and cheer.

Ah, there it is! What a pleasant glow!
Dear Rose is watching for me, I know;
I'm a happy man, though I own no lands,
And work from morn until night with my hands.
Is Rose at her knitting? Is Boy asleep?
Close to the window I softly creep,

And my own little heaven on earth I see.
The kettle is singing right merrily,
The fire sends out its ruddiest glow,
And supper waits on a cloth of snow;
While Rose, still fairer than when we were wed,
Sits rocking our boy in his cradle bed.

God bless them both! but what ails my sight?
I hadn't noticed this mist to-night.
She has caught my step, she opens the door!
Forgotten the burdensome way travelled o'er;
For two dear arms uplifted I see,
And Rose, my Rose, is welcoming me!

To Woman who Toileth.

PLACE a spray in thy belt, or a rose on thy stand,
　　When thou settest thyself to a commonplace
　　　seam;
Its beauty will brighten the work in thy hand,
　　Its fragrance will sweeten each dream.

When life's petty details most burdensome seem,
　　Take a book — it may give thee the peace thou
　　　hast sought —
And turn its leaves o'er, till thou catchest the gleam
　　Of some gem from the deep mine of thought,

When the task thou performest is irksome and long,
  Or thy brain is perplexed by a doubt or a fear,
Fling open the window, and let in the song
  God hath taught to the birds for thy cheer.

And lean from the casement a moment, and rest.
  While the winds cool thy cheek, glance thou up
    at the sky,
Where the cloud-ships are sailing, like argosies
    blest,
  Bright-winged and with majesty by.

Then steal a fair picture of mountain or glen —
  A smooth-gliding streamlet, through green mead-
    ows sweet;
Or, if thy lot's cast midst the dwellings of men,
  Of some radiant face in the street.

Then carry it back to thy work, and perchance
  'T will remind thee of childhood, or sweetly recall
Some long-faded page of thy youthful romance, —
  It may be, the dearest of all.

Oh, a branch of wild-roses the barrenest ledge
  Maketh fit for a throne; while the blossoming vine
Will turn to a bower the thorniest hedge;
  So will beauty make stern life divine.

The Land Where We All Have Been.

I know of a land where we all have been,
    Yet never may go again,
Though we're women as brave as ever were seen,
    Or the biggest and strongest of men.

In this wonderful land of which I sing,
    We never knew toil or care;
For someone stood ready to fetch and bring,
    And we were the rulers there.

Though we wore no crowns of gold or flowers,
    We were kings and queens by right;
And the homage of love was always ours,
    From our subjects, day and night.

Our royal robes were embroidered with skill,
    Our beds were silken and soft ;
We lived in ease, and we had our will,
    And we rode in our carriages oft.

Whatever we did, the livelong day
    We were watched by admiring eyes ;
And whatever we said, or did n't say,
    We were thought to be wondrous wise.

And no matter how peevish or cross we grew,
    Or what tyrants we became,
There was one, at least, who loved us so true,
    That she worshipped us just the same ;

And if we were ill, or beset by fears,
    She would tend us with gentlest hand,
And soothe us by crooning sweet songs in our ears ;
    For we lived in Babyland.

Oh God, forgive us our tyranny there;
   And reward, where'er they may be,
The patient and loving souls, whose care
   Was ours in our infancy!

The Cradle in which John Quincy Adams was Rocked.*

To and fro, to and fro,
This queer little cradle used to go,
A hundred and twenty-five years ago.

Then, as now, 't was devoid of grace;
No dainty frills of silk and lace
Softened the light on the baby's face.

But the baby slept and ate and grew,
And laughed and cried and prattled and crew,
Just as babies nowadays do;

*On Exhibition at the World's Fair.

While the cradle was gently, lovingly swung,
To hymns by the fair young mother sung,
And the patriot father o'er it hung,

With a prayer on his lips for his infant son.
They were godly folk. All was prayerfully done,
In those reverent days of Washington.

In England, King George sat on his throne
And fancied these colonies all his own.
Ah, could he have better the colonists known!

He taxed and oppressed them ; and every hour
Made them feel the weight of a tyrant's power,
And sent over servants to make them cower.

All day the soldiers of the crown,
The British redcoats, up and down,
Tramped through the streets of Boston town.

And the babe that in this cradle lay
Was startled from sleep at break of day,
When their fifes and drums began to play;

But at eve he was held at the window to see
The patriots called Sons of Liberty,
While they sang of a time when the land should
    be free.

And the cradle hardly had been outgrown
When the boy, his mother's hand clasping his
    own,
Harked to the cannon's thunder and groan

From Bunker Hill; and, with flashing eye,
Saw the smoke clouds gather and mount on high,
And flaming Charlestown light the sky.

But the glad day came when the nation was free,
And he thanked his God upon bended knee,
And he cheered for the Union and Liberty.

Then the bells rang out, and the arms of the crown
Were torn from the wall of the Statehouse
    down,
And burned in the street in Boston town.

The boy to a noble manhood grew,
And toiled for his country his whole life through,
With honor unswerving, courageous, and true,

Till, his strength and his years in her service
    spent,
Aweary, the Old Man Eloquent
Sank at his post, sighing, "I am content."

But the little cradle stands to-day
Where thronging people may touch it and say:
"Here once that high-souled statesman lay!"

The Children's Saint.

Could you but peep into this home,
    I'm sure you'd say 't was cosy;
For sweet-voiced birds and blooming vines,
    And child-flowers gay and rosy,
Make summer life and joy within,
    Though winter winds are blowing;
And not less brightly glows the grate
    If leaden skies are snowing.

Dear grandmamma, in cap of lace,
   And kerchief smoothly fitting,
With graceful hand and placid face,
   Sits knitting, knitting, knitting, —
A tiny sock for baby Ray,
   Who at her feet is playing;
And Ritchie, in the easy-chair,
   In mamma's furs, goes sleighing.

Wee Annie, from her china cup,
   Her own pet kitten's feeding;
Sweet Mabel, womanly of mien,
   The latest tale is reading;
And mother trims a little gown,
   That's marvelously pretty;
While Aunt Amelia makes a sketch
   Of Annie and her kitty.

Upon the walls are pictures hung:
  Landscapes, with mild-eyed cattle;
An ancestor in puffs and frills;
  A knight equipped for battle;
A vanished friend; a sweet-faced child;
  A well-belovèd pastor;
And saints and cherubs, drawn, perhaps,
  By some forgotten master.

Down from those dim and hovering shapes,
  With halo-circled faces,
I look to her whose patient life
  Is spent in common places;
Whose daily round of toil and care
  None know save those beside her,
Who'll bravely do the task at hand
  Though joy or woe betide her,

Will fashion tiny coat and gown
    With swift and loving fingers;
Will break the bread for little mouths,
    And wipe the tear that lingers;
Will watch in sickness, guide in health, —
    This tenderest of mothers!
Oh is not *she* the Children's Saint
    Outshining all the others?

WITH THE CHILDREN.

Santa Claus's Sister.

WE stood at a crowded counter,
    Little Geraldine and I.
There was only a day before Christmas,
    And hundreds were waiting to buy.

The shelves and the cases were covered,
    And the counters were piled up high,
With the loveliest things for presents,
    Ever seen by a mortal eye.

There were books with most beautiful pictures,
    And the strangest, most wonderful toys,
That were brought from over the ocean,
    On purpose for girls and boys.

There were dolls that could waltz and play tennis,
  In dresses of satin and silk;
And horses to wind and set trotting,
  And cows that you really could milk.

There were dogs that could bark like the live ones,
  And birds of most brilliant wing,
With springs hid away 'neath their feathers,
  That would make them fly upward and sing.

But the eyes of the child who stood by me
  Had wandered away from all these, —
And the sparkling Christmas angels
  And the miniature Christmas trees, —

And were scanning the faces about us —
  The people that huddled and pressed,
And looked weary and cross with the struggle
  Of pushing in front of the rest;

And, grasping my hand, she whispered,
  With eager, childish grace,
" Oh, that must be Santa Claus' sister,
  She 's got such a Christmas face ! '

I looked where her glance had lighted ;
  And, lo ! in a threadbare gown,
Stood a queer little bent old woman,
  With a face all wrinkled and brown.

But the eyes that beamed out from it
  Were radiant with love and joy,
As, from all the beautiful objects,
  She chose one poor, cheap toy.

And the worn, brown face was illumined
  With a smile of good-will toward men,
That said, more plainly than language,
  She was keeping Christmas then.

I glanced at the forms about me !
 There were women in rich attire,
Whose unearned gold might purchase
 Fulfilment of each desire.

There were those of delicate feature,
 Of gentle breeding and race ;
But the queer little bent old woman
 Had the only Christmas face.

In shame, from my own I hastened
 To smooth the impatience and frown,
As I looked at Santa Claus' sister,
 In her faded threadbare gown ;

And I blessed both the child and the woman,
 For their Christmas sermon sweet,
As I pressed through the throng of shoppers,
 And into the crowded street.

A Wedding in the Garden.

Lady Rose and Sweet William were married last night,
  With Jack-in-the-pulpit to tie the knot tight;
Mary Gold for the bridesmaid, in flutings of yellow, —
  Wild Basil as groomsman, a really fine fellow!

Oh the Blue Bells rang chimes; and the Trumpet-flower blew
  All the glad strains of music his jovial heart knew;
And the Man-in-the-moon sent them down his best light,
  And smiled as he gazed on the beautiful sight.

All the Lilies were there, in their white fragrant
    gowns;
  And the Sunflowers stately, with great golden
    crowns;
And the graceful young Poppy, in red satin frock;
  And the Foxglove and Larkspur and grand
    Hollyhock;

And the pretty Sweet Pea, and the dear Mignonette,
  And a score more of beauties, whose names I
    forget;
For the guests were as many as found garden room.—
  There were youth, lovely faces, light, joy, and
    perfume!

When Jack-in-the-pulpit had made his adieu,
   Just after the grand wedding-supper was through,
The brave Lady's Slipper, who 'd walked from the wood,
   Saying she was created to dance, and she should,

Tiptoed to the music; and all followed suit, —
   Keeping time to the Trumpet-flower's merry toot-toot, —
From the Pansies, in velvets of every rich hue,
   To the Monkshood arrayed in his cowl of dull blue.

And the Primrose, forgetting her prudishness quite,
   Declared that to dance was but natural and right,
So joined in the waltz; and, what do you think?
   The Bachelor Button, with Old Betty Pink,

Went whirling around; and the sad Mourning
  Bride
 Was forgetting her grief, with the gay London
  Pride;
When the Poppy grew sleepy, and nodded good-
  night;
 Which broke up the party, and all took their
  flight.

Lady Marie's Mishap.

Over the ploughed ground, into the clover,
Ralph and wee Jessie, Marie and Rover,
Fly like a whirlwind. What are they doing?
Why are they there, and what mischief is brewing?

Our Ralph is just seven, a brave manly fellow,
With eyes blue and laughing, and locks of bright
    yellow.
Wee Jessie 's his sister, she 's four and a quarter,
With brown eyes, and tresses like shadowy water.

And Marie's a lady, who's come straight from Paris,
And crossed the wide ocean with Aunt Helen Harris.
She can't yet speak English, though surely she's
    learning,
For she looks very bright and she seems quite
    discerning.

She is fair as a lily!—may sunshine ne'er tan her!—
And we greatly admire the repose in her manner.
Like her own native language, she speaks Greek and
    Latin.
And she's brought a whole trunkful of gowns made
    of satin.

Unaccustomed to walking through ploughed ground
    or clover,
She rides on the back of dear faithful old Rover;
And Ralph, the young beau,—Hear him cheering
    and calling!—
Has his arm round her shoulder, to keep her from
    falling,

Oh dear me! What's the matter? Old Rover, disgracing
His age and position, is bounding and racing,
And barking at swallows. Shame, shame! naughty Rover!
There lies Lady Marie, face down in the clover.

Oh run and get water! I fear she is dying!
Oh how she must suffer! How still she is lying!
Go quick, bring a doctor,— one skilful in healing!
No! see! she bleeds sawdust,— a doll without feeling!

Giving.

Lady Rose, Lady Rose,
    In your fragrant furbelows,
You give the winds sweet messages,
    Whichever way it blows;
You send them to the stranger,
    You send them to your friend;
From out your store of treasure,
    To other lives you lend.

Little bird, little bird,
   As you sing upon your bough,
A hundred hearts are happier
   That you are singing now;
Though the sun is shining brightly,
   Or is hiding in a cloud,
You give the world your sweetest songs,
   And sing them brave and loud.

Merry brook, merry brook,
   As you dance upon your way,
The rose had not the heart to bloom,
   Were you not here to-day,
Nor could a thirsty birdling trill
   Its songs so sweet and gay.
Oh, blessings to you, merry brook,
   As you dance upon your way!

Precious girls, precious boys,
    Know you not that you possess —
More than rose or bird or brook, —
    Gifts of cheer and loveliness?
Thoughts and words and deeds of love,
    Be you always freely giving,
And the world, with all who know you,
    Will be richer for your living.

If I Were a Boy Instead of a Girl.

"Oh, if I were a boy instead of a girl!"
Sighed little Kate Wrenn, as she shook back a curl,
And threw down her mending, and made a wry face,
"I'd stay out all day, and I'd run and I'd race.
And I'd pick lots of flowers, and I'd swing in the barn;
For I should n't have any old stockings to darn!
And I'd go down to Annie's, and take my doll Bess,
A'wearing my lovely new pink gingham dress.
Oh! how perfectly happy my days would all be,
If a pair of old stockings I never need see!"

"Ha ha, little sister!" laughed loudly Jack Wrenn,
"I guess you were n't thinking of what you said then;
For if you were a boy, though you had n't to sew,
You 'd find you had errands in plenty to go;
And you 'd have to make kindlers, pile wood, and rake hay,
Instead of just playing the whole livelong day.
And then, if you dressed like the boys of this town,
You 'd have to wear trousers, and not a pink gown;
And though you 'd have marbles, tops, ninepins and ball,
You would never have seen your fine dolly at all!"

"Deary me, that is true!" in horror, cried Kate,
As she caught up a sock. "What a terrible fate!
I just could n't live without my doll Bess!
And how dreadful 't would be, to lose my pink
 dress,—
And my blue one, and white, and all of the rest!
And how awkward and queer I should feel, to be
 drest
In jacket and trousers!—and then, to pile wood,
And make kindlers!—Oh! really, I do n't think
 I could!
And I do n't care one penny for your kind of
 toys;
Oh I 'm glad I 'm a girl, and I pity the boys!"

The Prisoner of the Snow Fort.

It was cloudy at even, it stormed all night,
And when morning came the world was white;
And the snow lay deep over hill and plain.
"Hurrah!" cried the boys, "we'll to battle again!"

So they built a great fort, of snowballs packed hard,
And they placed in its walls a valiant guard;
Then the rest of the boys — they called themselves men —
Rushed gallantly up again and again.

The fort was entered, and bravely won;
No lives had been lost when the battle was done;
But the soldier who stood at the entrance gate
Refused to kneel unto foe or fate.

So he was sentenced to stay without food,
A prisoner fast, till he was subdued.
And the conquerors walled the fort up tight,
And left him there in that pitiful plight.

No fire had he, not a crumb of bread;
No chair to sit down in, not even a bed.
He has wept every day, and been frozen each night;
And his face is as thin as a ghost's, and as white.

That battle was fought a week ago;
Yet he's prisoned there still, in that fort of snow.
You say it is cruel? Oh dear me, no!
For that is the man that they made of snow!

Kitty's Birthday Party.

Our Kitty is five years old to-day;
So she 's having a party, the very best way,
   Out under the great green trees.
She 's dressed all in white, and has flowers in her
    hand,
So even the birds overhead understand,
   And are singing our Kitty to please.

Five children in all! There is Kitty herself,
Who 's a gay little, queer little, frolicsome elf;
   And beside her, her big brother John.
Then there are her three little cousins from town,
In their muslins of rose-color, cream, and light
    brown,
   Named Alice and Grace and Mignonne.

The hammock is up; and in it there sit
John, Kitty, Grace, Alice — a very snug fit!
  And gently they sway to and fro;
While close to their feet — the sweet grass upon,
And weaving a beautiful wreath — is Mignonne;
  For Kitty must have one, you know.

John has brought out a table; it stands in the
    grass!
And after the treat has been spread, if you pass,
  And the children's acquaintance should make,
I think they 'd invite you to come take a seat,
And have strawberries and sherbet and bonbons
    to eat,
  And a slice of the birthday cake.

Birthday Letter.

DEAR FLOSSIE: I wish I might have something
    better,
To send for your birthday, than just a poor letter;
But I'll fill it with pictures, and write it in rhyme,
And find a gift nicer a year from this time.

And now, if some fairy would lend me her wand,
All the bright pretty playthings, of which you are
    fond,
Should fill your hands full, and o'erflow your small
    lap,
And then, when you woke from your very next nap,

The pair of fine ponies, you've longed for so,
Should stand at your door all ready to go.
And oh! when you went in your carriage to ride,
A sweet little sister should sit by your side,

And a coachman tiny, in livery gay,
Should drive you about all the livelong day;
While as dainty a footman as ever was seen
Should pay you the homage that's due to a queen.

How the ponies would prance! how their sleek
    sides would shine,
While the sunlight played over their harnesses fine!
The coachman's whip cracking,—how merry the
    sound!—
While ponies and carriage flew over the ground, —

And on o'er the roads to the city so bright!
How the people would stare, as you dashed into
sight,
With your liveried servants, ablaze in the sun,
In their buttons of gold! —Was there ever such fun?

Then out from the city, through village and lane,
On, on at full speed, lest the bright day should
wane,—
And on, like the wind, past mountain and shore,
And still on, till the long, happy day was all o'er,

And the earliest shadows of coming night,
Hid the earth, like a veil, from your sleepy sight.
Then you 'd homeward fly, as a bird to its nest,
To mamma's fond embrace — the true place for
rest.

But here I am listening, and listening in vain,
For the gentle tap on my door, or my pane,
Of the fairy coming her wand to lend;
So, alas! I have nothing but wishes to send.

But I would put my love in this letter to you,
But, as true as the sky that's above us is blue,
'T is so monstrous big,— you 'll believe it I hope?
That I can 't get it into the envelope.

The Child and the Aster.

The personified flowers in this poem belong to the Composite Family.

"Oh beautiful Aster!" a little maid cried,
"Please tell me, have some of your relatives died?
For when all else is gay," said the dear little girl,
"You Asters wear nothing but purples and pearl."

The frail Aster shivered. Pray was it a sigh,
Or naught but the breath of the wind passing by?
A bird twittered o'erhead, the brook rippled on;
But no word from the Aster the little maid won.

"The sumach is blazing by wayside and down;
On the hilltop the Goldenrod gleams like a crown!
The ripe ilex berries, all scarlet, I see,
And the ivy hangs red on the old apple-tree.

"Oh, the whole wood is burning with crimson and
    gold!
See! of gentians I 've found all my apron would
    hold.
Oh, when all else is gay," cried the sweet little girl,
"Pray why are you Asters in purples and pearl?"

The Aster shook sadly her delicate head.
"My child, you 've divined it," she falteringly said;
"Our family is broken; I 've watched, day by day,
My dearest of kin pass forever away.

"Oh, our race has known fame! Of its beauty and
    gold,
Over and over the poets have told.
To the cities great artists our pictures have borne;
But all that is past! Is it strange that I mourn?

"Now there were the Dandelions, wealthy and gay;
The sweet blue-eyed Chicories, down by the way;
The great brown-eyed Daisies, who lived on the hills;
And their cousins, more fair, in their dainty white frills;

"The Ragworts, that danced when the plowman's voice rang,
And who heard all the secrets the nesting birds sang;
And pretty Mayweed—she would live in the street;
And the Yarrows, whose fringes drooped over their feet.

"And now they're all gone! and the wind paused to say,
This morn as he came from the hills down this way,
That poor Thistle was dead; and he brought this soft strand
Of her silvery hair, to lay in my hand.

"And Goldenrod 's aging, his plumes are less gay;
And I and my sisters may go any day.
E'en our Sunflower is fading; God bless her bright
 face!
Our family has called her the Queen of the Race.

"And now that we Asters are almost alone,
  Do you wonder, dear child," — low and sad was
    her tone, —
"That we 're clad, as you see, all in purples and
    pearl?"
Tears stood in the eyes of the kind little girl.

But a moment they gleamed, then her bright, sunny
    smile
Had dried them all up, and she answered mean-
    while:
"Fair Aster, sweet Aster, pray do not grieve so,
Your friends are not dead. Oh, do you not know,

"That the flowers, now drooping on earth's loving
    breast,
Have only lain down for their long winter's rest?
They will sleep, 'neath the cover the snow-angels
    spread,
As snugly and warm as a child in its bed;

"And all the late autumn and bleak winter through,
They will dream of green fields and skies of soft
    blue,
Till the robin's note rings through the wood and
    the glen
To wake them to life; then they'll all bloom again."

My Little Milkmaid.

Though the winds may roar and the rains may pour,
Each morning I hear, when the clock strikes four,
A step 'neath my window, — a clink at my door.
Then I know, in the corner, there stands a bright can
Of the creamiest milk that ever there ran,
With a musical drip, into pail or pan.
"Who brings it?" you ask. " 'T is the milkman's task,
Or perhaps his boy's," you confident cry;
But you are mistaken, and so was I,
Till I peered through the blind, one morning, to find
(And 't was such a surprise I scarce trusted my eyes)
That the bounding step was a stout little girl's!
She had merry brown eyes and red-gold curls,—

This brave little maiden, with cans of milk laden,—
And went dancing along with a snatch of sweet song,
As gay as the robin that sang overhead;
While I, in bewilderment, crept back to bed;
But next morning I cried, when her form I espied:
"Can it be it is you, who all summer through
Have been bringing me milk, so sweet and so new?"
And she laughed, and said "Yes! Pray did n't you guess
That a girl could bring milk just as well as a boy?"
And with nod and with smile, that were pretty and coy,
She bade me adieu, ran the garden gate through,
And was gone, with her curls and her cap of bright blue.

How They Started for the Fair.

He.
  I wish I owned a ship, miss!
    Then out to sea we 'd go,
  And find a bran-new country,
    As Columbus did, you know.
  Of course I 'd be the cap'n;
    But you could be the mate;
  And when I came to glory,
    Why, you should share my fate.
  Of course I 'd be the king there,
    And have a golden throne;
  But I 'd make you queen, and give you
    A pearl crown for your own.
  Or had I but a carriage,
    I 'd take you out to ride!
  Of course I 'd drive the ponies,
    But you 'd sit by my side.

She.
    'T is true you have no carriage,
      Or ship or golden throne;
    But there 's that tandem 'cycle,
      And is n't it your own?

He.
    I never thought of that, miss!
      Jump on, and we will spin,
    Until we reach Chicago,
      And to the Fair have been.

    She jumped upon the 'cycle,
      He sprang to his seat, too;
    The wheels were set in motion,
      And off they quickly flew!

Helping Zeke.

A Day in Webster's Boyhood.

Midst New Hampshire's hills of granite,
    Ere the century was born,
Stood a farmhouse; and about it
    Lay the pleasant fields of corn.

Here Judge Webster, judge and farmer,
    Dwelt in peace, and tilled his land,
While his two sons, Zeke and Daniel,
    Lent to him a helping hand.

Two fine boys were Zeke and Daniel,
    Destined to be famous men,
And to win and merit honors
    Which they never dreamed of then.

Little thought the youthful Daniel,
   As he barefoot raked the hay,
Of the orator and statesman
   He would find himself, one day,—

Dreamed not, as his bright eyes sparkled,
   'Neath his straw hat's broken brim,
Of the chaplet fair, of oak-leaves,
   That the years would weave for him.

On a bright midsummer morning,
   When the meadow grass was down,
Came a message for the farmer,
   Calling to a neighboring town.

So he went, with strong injunctions
   That the boys should work, not play,—
Do the weeding in the garden,
   Turn and rake the meadow hay.

Oh the air was full of sweetness!
    Pleasant was the sunshine's glow,
On that glad midsummer morning,
    More than fourscore years ago.

Danced the boys' hearts in their bosoms,
    As the brook danced 'neath the trees;
Every vine its wealth of blossoms
    Flung like banners to the breeze.

Every lily in the meadow
    Noiseless rang its golden bells;
As the heart, when joy is fullest,
    All its joy in silence tells.

Hummed the bees among the clover;
    And the gay-winged butterfly,
With its light and airy motion,
    Flitted through the azure sky.

Sang the birds in blithesome chorus,
  As no birds ere sang before;
Brighter seemed the redbreast's feathers
  Than a redbreast ever wore.

Gayly frisked the little chipmunk,
  Peering down with saucy face,
Venturing nearer, springing backward,
  Tempting to a merry chase.

Strawberries ripened 'mong the fern-leaves,
  On the margin of the brook,
In whose depths the speckled beauties
  Waited for the farm-boy's hook.

Hung the cherries, red and luscious,
  In the tree, right overhead.
Could a boy leave all these treasures, —
  Just to weed an onion-bed?

Sped the day. The joyous hours,
  One by one, had all been told;
And the great sun, slowly sinking,
  Dipped into a sea of gold.

Only on a far-off hilltop
  Fell its last rays, like a crown,
When the old judge — home returning
  From his long day in the town —

Found no weeds had been uprooted,
  In the garden on the hill;
While the corn, that should be grinding,
  Was not carried to the mill.

Lay the long swaths in the meadow,
  As at sunrise they were laid —
When the dew was thick upon them —
  By the mower's shining blade.

Though the morrow was the Sabbath,
   And the hour already late,
Still the kine, with heavy udders,
   Waited at the pasture gate.

"What does all this mean?" he questioned,
   "What has happened here to-day?
Boys, what have you done since morning?
   Have you worked, or did you play?"

As in silence they looked downward:
   "Come my lads, why do n't you speak?"
"I 've been doing nothing, father!"
   With contrition, murmured Zeke.

Turning to the embryo statesman:
   "Pray, what have you done, young man?"
While his dark eyes brimmed with laughter,
   "I 've helped Zeke, sir," answered Dan.

Bessie's Riches.

Oh, do you know our Bessie?
  She's rich as any queen,
Though stately hall or palace
  She never once has seen;
Though gown of lace or satin,
  She may not call her own,
And silk or ermine mantle
  Ne'er round her form is thrown;

Though not a diamond has she,
  To sparkle on her hand,
No waiting-maid or footman,
  To fly at her command;
Though neither plate nor jewels
  Will e'er be hers, I ween,
Or lands or lofty title,
  She's rich as any queen!

Oh pray, where are her riches?
   Of what do they consist?
Has she a wit, whose sparkle
   No mortal can resist?
Or does her gold lie prisoned
   Within her shining hair?
Or has her face rare beauty,
   And does her wealth lie there?

Nay, though her wit is merry,
   'T is naught to make one vain;
Although her hair is sunny,
   No gold does it contain;
And, though her face is winsome,
   Her beauty's in her smile,
And in the sweet directness
   Of a glance all free from guile.

Her wealth is greater, rarer,
  Than wit or beauty's dower!
Wit fails to render happy;
  Beauty but has its hour;
The riches she possesses,
  Our joyous little Bess,
Lie in the golden sunshine
  Of a heart's unselfishness.

The May Party.

DIRECTIONS.

THE stage should be carpeted with green, and strewn with flowers. It would be pretty to have boughs or small trees arranged at the back of the stage so as to cover the wall. Upon these boughs two or three straw hats, trimmed with wreaths or bright-colored ribbons, should be carelessly hung. The number of children, among whom should be a few little boys, need be limited only by the size of the stage, care, of course, being taken that they are not huddled or crowded. Very small children, who cannot sing, may be introduced, with pleasing effect, in grouping.

The throne, which, in scenes first and second, occupies the centre of the stage, can be easily arranged by using empty boxes, covered with bright shawls and sofa-cushions. In scene second an arch of flowers should be held over the queen. It can be a barrel-hoop, wound with leaves and flowers. The end should be held, on either side, by a little boy dressed in page's costume. The crown should be placed upon the head of the queen by the first maid of honor, immediately after the five have recited their verses. As soon as the crown has been adjusted, the sceptre should be handed to the queen by the second maid of honor.

At the moment when the crown is placed upon the head of the queen each girl should raise a simple wreath of flowers to her own head, where it should remain through scenes second and third.

The dresses of all the girls may be white, with bright sashes, or trimming of flowers; or, for variety, some may wear thin dresses of gay colors.

At the close of the second scene the throne is carried from the stage, and the maypole substituted, ready for scene third. The maypole should be adorned at top and base with wreaths. If the ribbons are not to be braided by the children, the pole should be wreathed with flowers its entire length, and the ribbons dispensed with; in which case the children should form two circles about the pole, one within the other, and the circles should move in opposite directions. Of course the children should keep perfect time to the music.

In scene first the children should be in natural groups at the front of the stage, and about the empty throne, some standing, some sitting, winding wreaths or arranging bouquets. Between scenes first and second the groups should be broken up and new ones formed.

Each maid of honor carries a garland or bouquet, composed of the flowers mentioned in her verse. These garlands and bouquets are to be handed to the queen as soon as she has received her crown and sceptre. As there will be more than she can gracefully receive in hand or lap, they may be placed on her shoulders, the throne, or at her feet. The queen is seated on the throne when scene second opens.

Any other tunes than the ones indicated, if familiar and sprightly, may be used for the songs.

SCENE I.

OPENING SONG.

(To be sung by all.)

Tune: Oh Swiftly Glides our Bonny Boat.

WITH hearts as light as thistledown,
 We meet upon this green,
With feet that all impatient wait
 To dance about our queen.

But who, among the merry group,
 Shall sit upon our throne,
And wear the crown of flowerets bright,
 The sweetest ever blown?

Oh, wise and gentle, passing fair,
  Our gracious queen must be;
With heart and hand unsullied as
  The pure anemone.

With lips whose sunny smile betrays
  A nature warm and true,
And eyes her subjects' griefs can turn
  To violets wet with dew.

Oh who, of all this merry group,
  Shall sit upon our throne,
And wear the crown of flowerets bright,
  The sweetest ever blown?

SCENE II.

CROWNING THE QUEEN.

Tune: When the Day with Rosy Light.

Ere the golden beams of morning
  From her slumbers waked the dell,
While the birds their matins mingled
  With the sound of pasture bell,

Roamed we over hill and valley,
  Through the wood and meadow green,
Culling flowers both bright and fragrant,
  Flowers to deck our Mayday queen.

The next five verses are to be recited in turn by the five maids of honor.

1.   HASTENED I unto the meadow;
        There, above the rich brown mold,
    Myriad cowslips caught the sunbeams,
        In their shining cups of gold.

2.   Wandered I beside the brooklet;
        There, beneath my springing feet,
    Violets, white and blue and purple,
        Made each passing zephyr sweet.

3.   Fair hepaticas I gathered,
        On the brow of yonder hill,
    And Cassandra's dainty bell-flowers
        Found I by the ruined mill.

4.   Clambered I o'er roughest ledges,
        Lichen-painted, gray with age,
    Where the columbine glowed scarlet,
        By the snowy saxifrage.

5.   'Neath the pines whose swaying branches
       Make low music overhead,
    Found I wind-flowers, pale and fragile,
       Where arbutus had blushed red.

These two verses may be recited by one of the maids of honor, or sung by them all together, as one girl crowns the queen.

    TAKE our offerings, gracious sovereign,
       Violet, pink, anemone;
    Wear the crown, accept the garlands,
       We have fondly twined for thee.

    May thy reign be bright and joyous,
       Light the burdens thou shalt bear;
    May thy heart contain no sorrow,
       And thy crown no thorn of care.

THE QUEEN'S REPLY.

GRATEFULLY, my little maidens,
   Will I take the garlands fair ;
Eagerly I 'll strive, and always,
   To be worth the love ye bear.

And as May, the radiant goddess,
   Gems our way with brightest flowers,
So, with mirth and joy and gladness,
   Will I crown your passing hours.

Now before the shadows lengthen,
   Ere the night draws on apace,
Let the sounds of dance and chorus
   Echo through this sylvan place.

SCENE III.

THE MAYPOLE DANCE.

The music and dancing are heard before the children are seen. The rising curtain discloses the dance in progress, when the verse has been sung once; after which, without any pause, it is repeated once or twice; that is, long enough to make the scene of satisfactory length. The curtain should fall while the tableau is still moving.

Tune: Lightly Row.

CHORUS.

HERE we go, here we go,
Tripping lightly to and fro,
Round and round, round and round,
With the queen we 've crowned.
While the brooklet yonder seen,
While the shadows on the green,
Dance and glide, dance and glide,
Dance we side by side.

Arbor-Day Song.

GREENLY grow, oh trees we 've planted,
  May your fair leaves multiply,
And the nesting song-birds yearly
  To your spreading branches fly.

Crown the landscape with your beauty;
  Freely give your fruit and shade;
Make ten thousand hearts more happy,
  For the efforts we have made!

Heaven send you showers and sunshine,—
  Spare from gale and lightning stroke;
And may winter, while he 's reigning,
  Wrap you in his ermine cloak.

IN LIGHTSOME MOOD.

Our Christmas.

WE did n't have much of a Christmas,
  My papa and Rosie and me,
For mamma 'd gone out to the prison,
  To trim up the poor prisoners' tree;
And Ethel, my big grown-up sister,
  Was down at the 'sylum all day,
To help at the great turkey dinner,
  And teach games for the orphans to play.
She belongs to a club of young ladies,
  With a " beautiful object," they say;
'T is to go among poor, lonesome children,
  And make all their sad hearts more gay.

And auntie (You do n't know my auntie?
  She's my own papa's half-sister Kate!)
She was 'bliged to be round at the chapel
  Till 't was — oh, some time dreadfully late;

For she pities the poor worn-out curate,
   His burdens, she says, are so great;
So she 'ranges the flowers and the music,
   And he goes home around by our gate.
I should think this way must be the longest,
   But then, I suppose he knows best;
Aunt Kate says he intones most splendid;
   And his name is Vane Algernon West.

My papa had bought a big turkey,
   And had it sent home Christmas Eve;
But there was n't a soul here to cook it;
   You see Bridget had threatened to leave
If she could n't go off with her cousin,
   (He does n't look like her one bit!)
She says she belongs to a union,
   And the union won't let her submit;
So we ate bread and milk for our dinner,
   And some raisins and candy; and then
Rose and me went down stairs to the pantry,
   To look at the turkey again.

Papa said he would take us out riding;
   Then he thought that he did n't quite dare,
For Rosie 'd got cold and kept coughing,—
   There were dampness and chills in the air.
Oh, the day was so long and so lonesome,
   And our papa was lonesome as we;
And the parlor was dreary— no sunshine!
   And all the sweet roses, the tea
And the red ones — and ferns and carnations,
   That have made our bay window so bright,—
Mamma 'd picked for the men at the prison,
   To make their bad hearts pure and white.

And we all sat up close to the window,
   Rose and me on our papa's two knees,
And we counted the dear little birdies
   That were hopping about on the trees.
Rosie wanted to be a brown sparrow,
   But I thought I would rather, by far,
Be a robin that flies away winters,
   Where the sunshine and gay blossoms are.

And papa wished he was a jailbird,
   'Cause he thought that they fared the best;
But we all were real glad we were n't turkeys,
   For then we 'd been killed with the rest.

That night I put into my praying:
   "Dear God, we 've been lonesome today;
For mamma, aunt, Ethel, and Bridget,
   Every one of them all went away.
Won't you please make a club, or society,
   'Fore it 's time for next Christmas to be,
To take care of philanterpist's families,
   Like papa and Rosie and me?"
And I think that my papa 's grown pious,
   For he listened as still as a mouse,
Till I got to Amen, then he said it;
   So it sounded all over the house.

The Mugwump.

*The mugwump is an eastern bird,
With plumes of gorgeous hue;
His crest is red, his bosom white,
His wings celestial blue.*
     DR. WILLIAM EVERETT.

THOUGH all the ornithologists,
 That ever bagged a bird,
Should claim the mugwump for their own,
 I still should doubt their word.

The mugwump's a chameleon,
 Of ever-varying hue,
Whose color's stolen from the scene
 It chances to pass through.

When through the wood of ignorance,
 It rash and stumbling fled
(Leaving the Good Old Party)
 The Democrats to wed,

Its color (doubt it, you who will!)
   Was, naturally, green;
And of a tint as vivid
   As ever yet was seen.

But now, flung o'er it from the dawn
   Of late-seen truths, a hue
Creeps from its nose down to its tail,
   Which much resembles blue.

The Jealous Ghost.

One winter's night, a merry group,
    We watched the hearthfire glow;
While wildly raged the storm without,
    And drifted deep the snow.

It dashed against the window-pane,
    Heaped high the oaken sill;
And whirled in clouds across the lawn,
    And down the barren hill.

Yet swift the stream of converse flowed;
    While on its surface broke
Those laughter-bubbles, now and then,
    That mirth and jest evoke.

And all unheeded sped the hours,
   Whose wings no shadows cast,
Until, with pinions slightly drooped,
   The midnight hour lagged past;

And laugh and song were more subdued,
   And chat less merry grew;
The flames that lapped the smouldering log
   Had turned to spectral blue.

The storm was spent; the wind, grown hoarse,
   Was only heard to moan;
While, struggling through the drifting clouds,
   A young moon faintly shone

On whitened twigs of leafless trees,
   That ceaseless tapped the pane, —
As fingers of a ghost, that seeks
   Some entrance hard to gain;

And, gazing through the shadeless sash,
  Out on the snowclad night,
Fantastic forms seemed moving, in
  The pale moon's fitful light.

Forgotten now are men and things,
  The books upon the shelves;
And conversation straightway turns
  To goblins, ghosts, and elves.

And each his tale of horror pours
  Upon the listening ear,
Till our own shadows, on the wall,
  Strange phantom shapes appear, —

To all save one, of stronger nerve,
  (It is our youthful host)
Who still avers that he, for one,
  Should like to see a ghost.

Darker it grows! The pale blue flames
    Scarce show the flower-strewn rugs,
While all the air is quickly filled
    With subtle scent of drugs.

The candles have each flickered out;
    The moon is in a cloud.
Lo! in our midst a spectre stands,
    Draped in a long white shroud.

From out the caverns of his eyes
    Shoot tongues of greenish fire;
His bony hand clasps tight a wand,
    Set thick with many a brier.

Incongruous is the robe, or shroud,
    Which round his gaunt form curls;
For, while it savors of the grave,
    'T is richly fringed with pearls.

He turns upon our trembling host.
   His low, sepulchral tones
Are echoed by the dying wind,
   Which faintly wails and moans.

"From out the land of shades came I,
   Long have I wandered here,
Seeking in vain, until tonight,
   To gain a human ear,

"That I might give unto the world
   The story of my wrongs;
And claim the wreath another wears,
   That on my brow belongs.

"Men make great feasts to Hahnemann,
   They speak his name with awe;
Sacred his memory to the world,
   His lightest whim a law;

"While I, from whom he stole those truths,
  On which rests all his fame,
Have been forgotten, or ignored,
  And none have heard my name.

" Similia similibus
  Curantur," mutters he !
" Know ye I was the pioneer
  In Homœopathy.

" I was the man" (his eyes dilate,
  His tones to thunder rise)
" Who jumped into a bramble bush,
  And scratched out both his eyes;"

(A groan, as if he still recalls
  The agonizing pain)
" Then jumped into another bush,
  And scratched them in again."

His errand done, our curious guest
    Seems meditating flight ;
But, ere the apparition strange
    Has vanished from our sight,

The wasted hearth-log breaks and falls,
    A bright flame leaps and curls,
And flings its light across the fringe,
    We thought was made of pearls,

Which borders deep the ornate gown,
    And droops from all its frills ;
And lo! our fancied pearls are naught
    But tiny sugar pills.

Andrea's Discovery.

We sat and talked of storied days,
  Of men whose lives were brave and bold;
Then of the minstrels, whose sweet lays
  Their deeds of chivalry have told.

And one cried out : " How strange a thing,
  That human speech should fall in rhyme !
And that the words our poets sing
  Should smoothly flow in measured time. "

Another sought the laws that be,
  Whereby a rhythmic tale is told,
And fain would find some recipe
  By which a poem would unfold.

And, knowing I must guilty plead
    To writing out, from time to time,
In homespun phrase, for folk to read,
    Some simple verse, or tale in rhyme,

With one accord they turned to me,
    And cried : " Pray, if you can, explain
This ever-baffling mystery ! " —
    But questioning me was all in vain.

When from the group I soon withdrew,
    And turned me to my desk to write,
A little maiden, three times two,
    Came after me on tiptoes light.

" Do let me stay ! I 'll be so good ! "
    She pleaded with a winsome laugh ;
And by my chair she silent stood,
    While click-clack went the calligraph.

As o'er the keys my fingers flew
　Her face a look bewildered wore,
Till from the roll came creeping through
　A leaf that printed verses bore.

At first the child amazed stood dumb;
　Then clapped her hands, and cried in glee:
"I know now how your poems come,—
　You make 'em with your 'chinery!"

The Usurer's Reply.

HERR BLUMENTHAL,—a Jew who dwelt
    Beside the pleasant Rhine,
Whose waters lave the feet of hills
    Crowned by the fruitful vine,—

With wealth possessed, and rightful gain,
    Could never be content;
So rented out his store of gold
    At nine, not six, percent.

"Herr Blumenthal," said one, "although
    You do our Christ deny,
You cannot for a moment doubt
    There is a God on high,—

"A God who sees all things you do,
  Down looking from above;
And can He bless a usurer,
  This God of right and love?"

The Jew, on parchment by his side,
  A bony finger laid,
And muttered, half beneath his breath,
  "Olt Isaac ist not vraidt.

"Mine Gott vill never know dot I
  Vor moneys sharge too tear;
Vor, ven he look from Himmel high,
  Down on dese vigures here,"

(And craftier smile ne'er lit the face
  Of Jew beside the Rhine),
"Dis vill to him appear a 6,
  Dot to our eyes ist 9."

Advice to a Despairing Lover.

Lover, sighing in despair,
All because a maiden fair
Deigneth not for thee to care,

Quit thy dreaming! List to me,
If I may thy mentor be;
There is still a chance for thee!

I 've a secret I 'll impart,
That will give to thee the art
Of winning this fair maiden's heart.

Rouse thyself! attention lend!
Every dart that lovers send
Hath a barb at either end.

When another shaft is thrown,
Keep thine own heart hard as stone;
' T will, rebounding, pierce her own.

When Pushed to the Wall.

If you 're harassed and hurried,
And driven and worried,
And given no quarter at all ;
If you 're wounded and grieved,
Traduced and deceived,
Till the nectar of life turns to gall ;

If you 're cheated and swindled,
Till, credit all dwindled,
You stand face to face with despair;
If beggars pursue,
And debts are o'erdue,
Till you scarce own the shoes that you wear ;

In short, if in spite
Of the manliest fight,
You find yourself pushed to the wall;
Do n't bang your head on it,
But sit down upon it,
And rest, ere you struggle at all.

GREETINGS.

An Old Old-Fashioned Flower.

To Whittier.

With gift of blossoms sweet and gay,
Dear poet, I would mark the day
   When you were sent the earth to cheer;
Yet feel, who dwells near nature's heart,
The flowers that bloom through human art,
   Than those God-given, would hold less dear.

But when without I turn my eye,
The naked branches 'gainst the sky,
   And fallen leaves that heap the ground,
Tell me that in no sheltered nook,
By woodland path or meadow brook,
   Is there one blossom to be found.

And vainly, too, within my mind
I look, some flower of thought to find,
   So newly bright, so freshly sweet,
That each word-petal seems to bear
A message rich and fine and rare,
   An offering for a poet meet.

So send I — I 've naught else — a flower,
That blooms as free when field and bower
   No longer bee and blossom know,
As when, to tunes the blithe birds sing,
Mid troops of flowers that dance and swing,
   The summer breezes come and go.

An old, old-fashioned flower, whose seed
The angels —'t is their sweetest deed! —
   Once scattered earthward from above;
And, rooting in men's hearts, it grew,
And blossoms still, the whole year through,—
   The old, old-fashioned flower of love.

November Greeting.

This morn I flung open my casement,
    As the day was beginning to wake.
"What means it?" I cried in amazement,
    As I watched the clouds kindle and break;

For the great sun came up in full splendor,
    The river reflected its glow,
And the blue skies were shining and tender,
    Like the eyes of a maiden I know.

"Why this glory," I cried, "in November?
    The world must be having a fête!"
But just then I chanced to remember,
    Or the calendar told me, the date.

Then the mystery lifted and vanished,
　As the clouds of the morning had done ;
All feelings of wonder were banished,
　For I knew 't was your birthday, dear one.

And the heavens had but smiled on their daughter,
　And rejoiced in the day of her birth ;
And their joy had been caught by the water,
　For her life had made sunshine on earth
.

Greeting with Bluebells.

WERE I the summer breeze, dear girl,
   And did each azure bell conceal
A silvery tongue of joyous tone,
   I 'd make them sound a merry peal.

I 'd madly play among the flowers,
   Each fairy bell I 'd toss and swing,
Until the echoes gave again
   The birthday chime I 'd gaily ring.

But since I 'm not the summer breeze,
   And since these bells may sound no chime,
I sing my love, my wishes kind,
   And send instead this simple rhyme,

Chime for September Wedding.

Heigh'o and heigh'o and o'heigh!
   So gay are your wedding-bells ringing,
Their echoes, in frolicking by,
   Have set all my rhyme-bells to swinging.

And the merriest music they know,
   With the chimes for your bridal shall mingle;
Heigh'o and o'heigh and heigh'o!
   Be you happier wedded than single!

Aurora, as soon as 't was day,
   From the sky hung a beautiful awning;
A sign be its rosy hues gay,
   Of the life that before you is dawning!

May the golden-rod, bright on the hill,
   Stand a pledge, in its wealth and its splendor,
Of the riches of love that shall fill
   Your hearts, be they loyal and tender!

And the beauty that's everywhere rife,
   This glorious month of September,
Prove a type of your union, till life
   Shall have burnt out its very last ember!

Heigh'o and heigh'o and o'heigh!
   So gay are your wedding-bells ringing,
Their echoes, in frolicking by,
   Have set all my rhyme-bells to swinging.

And the merriest music they know,
   With the chimes for your bridal shall mingle;
Heigh'o and o'heigh and heigh'o!
   Be you happier wedded than single!

Welcome to Baby.

Coming in the bright midsummer,
   When the blossoms deck the bowers,
Mayst thou, little heaven-sent treasure,
   Prove the fairest flower of flowers.

May the fates, thy future weaving,
   Hovering o'er thy dainty bed,
Make thy life-web one of beauty,
   Shower blessings on thy head, —

Fill thy heart with joy and sunshine,
   Keep thee free from all alarms,
As thou art when sweetly sleeping,
   In thy mother's loving arms.

TRANSLATIONS.

The Mountain Emigrant.

From the French of Chateaubriand.

How sweetly, as I dream, advance
The scenes that earliest met my glance!
  Ah sister, those were golden days,
Those days in France.
  My land, be thou my love always,
  My love always!

Canst still recall our mother's face?
And how, before the bright fireplace,
  She drew us evenings to her chair
With tender grace?
  And how we fondly stroked her hair,
  So long and fair?

Ah sister, dost thou see it all, —
The castle gray, whose moss-grown hall
   The bright Dore washed,— the Moorish tower,
With crumbling wall,
Whose ponderous bell, at sunrise hour,
   Rang out with power?—

The lake, that lay as if at rest,
While swallows skimmed its tranquil breast,—
   The breeze that swayed the rush, and tanned
Its bright brown crest, —
   The sinking sun, whose beauty grand
     Flushed wave and land?

And she, whose life lent joy to mine:
How oft the pretty flowering vine
   We 've sought beneath the old wood's shade,
Her hand in mine;
   Her cheek, as there we strayed,
     To mine was laid.

Ah, who 'll bring Helen back to me,—
My mountain grand, — the old oak tree?
  Their memory sweet, through all my days,
A pain must be!
  My land must be my love always,—
  My love always!

Carcassonne.

From the French of Gustave Nadaud.

I 'm sixty years, I 'm growing old ;
   Through all my days I 've wrought with care;
Yet never, as the seasons rolled,
   Has come fulfilment of my prayer.
I see, indeed, that while we live,
   Our bliss complete is never known ;
My heart's desire earth will not give;
   I never went to Carcassonne.

'T is dimly seen from yonder heights,
   Behind the hills that melt in blue;
And yet, to view its wondrous sights,
   Five weary leagues stretch out for you;
And to return, as many more.
   Ah, if the tardy grape were grown,
And all the work of vintage o'er! —
   I never shall see Carcassonne!

They tell me there 't is always gay,
   As Sundays are in little towns.
The people go about, they say,
   In fine new coats and spotless gowns.
And there one sees old castle walls,
   As grand as those of Babylon,—
A bishop and two generals!
   Alas, I know not Carcassonne!

The vicar 's right a hundred times ;
  He says we 're foolish, to our cost ;
And tells us, in his holy rhymes,
  That through ambition men are lost.
Yet could I manage, bye and bye,
  To find two days ere autumn 's flown !
Ah me ! how sweetly I could die,
  After I 'd gazed on Carcassonne !

My Heavenly Father, pardon me,
  If by my prayer I should offend !
Some joy beyond our grasp we see,
  From infancy unto life's end.
My good wife, with my son Aignon,
  Has travelled even to Narbonne ;
My grandson 's been to Perpignon,
  But I have not seen Carcassonne !

Thus crooned a peasant, near Limoux,
    A peasant bent with toil and age.
I said: "My friend, arise! With you
    I 'll go upon this pilgrimage."
When halfway there, while distance blue
    Still veiled the town he fain had known,
His journey on life's road was through!
    He never had seen Carcassonne!

The Ploughman and His Children.

From the French of La Fontaine.

Work with a will, work one and all!
Work is the stock that's least likely to fall.
A ploughman, whose lands were fertile and wide,
Feeling death was near, called his sons to his side.
"Guard your inheritance well," said he,
" Sell not this farm that my sires left me ;
For, concealed therein, a treasure lies ;
Know not I where 't is hid ; but unto your eyes
It shall be revealed, if you search with care.
Look when the harvesters leave the ground bare;
Rake and harrow and plough with pains,
Till not an unturned inch remains."
The father at rest, the sons to the fields
Went forth again ; but no gold was revealed,
Though they sought it well; but at the year's close
They found that their farm in value rose ;
For the father was wise : he had taught, ere he died,
That work is a treasure, whatever betide.

Child-times.

From the German of Heine.

My child, we were once little children,
    Merry and full of play;
We used to creep into the henhouse,
    And hide ourselves under the hay.

We cackled and craiked like the biddies;
    And then, when the people came by,
"Cocklededoo!" we shouted;
    And they thought it the cock's own cry.

Some boxes that stood in the courtyard,
    We carpeted over with care;
And at housekeeping there together,
    We played with the grandest air.

And the old cat, from the neighbor's,
   Came often a visit to pay;
And we courtesied and complimented,
   In a quaint and serious way;

And asked for her health politely,
   And how she felt each day.
Since then, to many old tabbies
   We 've talked the selfsame way.

Sometimes we sat sedately,
   Declaring, as grown folks do,
That the times had been far better,
   That we in childhood knew,—

That love and truth and religion
   Were vanishing off the earth.
We talked of the dearth of money,
   And how much coffee was worth.

All o'er are those childish fancies,
    And all things pass by like our youth,—
Our treasures, the world and its pleasures,
    And faith and love and truth.

The Castle by the Sea.

From the German of Uhland.

Hast thou seen the lofty castle,
  The castle by the sea?
The clouds are rose and golden,
  That float above it free.

It fain would cast itself downward,
  To the mirroring wave below;
And it fain would struggle upward,
  In the sunset's ruddy glow.

"Well have I seen that castle,
  The castle by the sea,
With the moon above it watching,
  While the mist rose shroudingly."

Did the wind and waves together
   Sing of joy, as they swept along?
Didst thou hear, from the lordly castle,
   Gay music and festival song?

"The wind and waves together
   Lay hushed in sadness deep,
While with tears I heard, from the castle,
   A bitter wailing sweep."

And sawest thou not the monarch,
   Or his stately wife behold,—
And the crimson mantles waving,
   And the crown of jewelled gold?

Led they not forth with rapture
   A royal maiden fair,
Radiant as the sunshine,
   With halo of golden hair?

"I saw indeed the parents;
  But without their jewels bright.
They were clad in sable garments,—
  No maiden was in sight."

IN THE SANCTUARY.

Easter Lilies.

Oh radiant lilies, of glistening white,
Rising majestic, blooming in light,
Breathing forth incense by day and by night!

If the tongues in your fair sweet bells have power,
Let them peal forth the tale, from this very hour,
Of the struggle from earth of each perfect flower.

Let them tell of the time when dormant you lay,
Far from the beauty and light of day,
In shroud-like wrappings, in cold dark clay.

Let them tell the story for those who deep
In graves of doubt and discouragement sleep,
Or who wrapped in the garments of selfishness keep;

And to those who till now have idly heard
The tidings of joy, and each beautiful word
That the dear Christ spoke; or are deterred

From breaking from darkness and seeking the
    light,
By their lack of faith in God's love and his might,
And so effortless lie in the gloom of night.

Tell them, by courage and striving and prayer,
That they too may rise to the sunlit air,
Where souls, like the lilies, bloom pure and fair;

And the words repeat, till they 're inward borne
Upon thousands of souls, this Easter morn,
Who shall upward strive and be newly born.

The Broader Field.

Oh thou who sighest for a broader field,
   Wherein to sow the seeds of truth and right,—
Who fain a fuller, nobler power would wield
   O'er human souls that languish for the light,—

Search well the realm that even now is thine!
   Canst not thou in some far-off corner find
A heart, sin-bound, like tree with sapping vine,
   Waiting for help its burdens to unbind?—

Some human plant, perchance beneath thine eyes,
   Pierced through with hidden thorns of idle fears;
Or drooping low, for need of light from skies
   Obscured by doubt-clouds, raining poison tears?—

Some bruisèd soul the balm of love would heal;
  Some timid spirit faith would courage give;
Or maimèd brother who, though brave and leal,
  Still needeth thee, to rightly walk and live?

Oh while one soul thou findst, which hath not known
  The fullest help thy soul hath power to give,
Sigh not for fields still broader than thine own;
  But, steadfast in thine own, more broadly live!

The Woodbird's Song.

Weary and sad one day,
I took my lonely way,
　Through meadows green,
Unto the wood where spread,
Around and overhead,
　A leafy screen.

There, in a mossy nook,
Beside a little brook,—
　That murmurs low
Its song of love and thanks
To flowers that on its banks
　In beauty grow,—

I laid me down to weep ;
It seemed my soul could keep
  No more its woe,
So hard my life had grown ;
For faith in God had flown,
  I thought; when, lo! —

From out the elder-bloom,
That lit the forest gloom
  Just overhead,
A bird's sweet song I heard,
Distinctly, every word ;
  And this it said:

"High in the bright blue sky,
Through sun and cloud I fly,
  Nor fear to fall.
Who taught me how to sing
Will strengthen my small wing;
  He cares for all, for all,—
  He cares for all.

"And, though I wander far,
Where pathless forests are,
　　Nor mark the way,—
Who me with birdlings blessed
Will guide me to my nest
　　At close of day, of day,—
　　At close of day."

The heaven-taught lay was hushed;
Then o'er my spirit rushed
　　A wave of joy,
That swept all doubt away,—
Brought faith, whose vital ray
　　Naught can destroy.

And while the brook, the breeze,
The birds and little bees,
　　On every side,
Voiced forth the woodbird's call,
"He cares for all, for all!"
　　I joyous cried:

"Who loves the birdling so,
Loves me far more, I know;
  I am His child.
And though I wander wide,
Where sin and woe betide,
  Despair is wild.

"For, surely, who will guide
The bird, at eventide,
  Unto her nest,
Will take me, when life's day
Shall fade in twilight gray,
  Back to His breast."

Not in that ancient book,
Where for His word we look,
  Alone He speaks;
But in each birdling's song,
Each wind that sweeps along,
  Our hearts He seeks,—

In each returning day
That, with its golden ray,
   Our slumber breaks,
In every springtime flower,
Foretelling autumn's dower,
   Fresh promise makes.

As homeward, from the wood,
I walked in happy mood,
   The nightbird's call,—
And crickets, round my way,
Loud chirping, — seemed to say,
   "He cares for all!"

While in my trusting heart,
A joy, that wealth or art
   Could never bring,
Thrilled through its very core,
And moved me o'er and o'er
   To softly sing:

"Oh surely, who will guide
The bird, at eventide,
  Unto her nest,
Will take me, when life's day
Shall fade in twilight gray,
  Back to His breast."

She is Not Dead.

Oh do not say, as one who knows not of
The blessèd gift called immortality,
That she who made life rich and sweet to me
Is taken from me, mine no more to be!
I have not lost her! Nay, still is she mine,
As when these arms encircled her dear form.
Her love—and is not that, in truth, herself?—
Is still mine own,— is, and will always be;
And time and space can lessen not its force.
She thinks of me, as I of her; and smiles,
When in her dreams we talk and laugh again,
As I in mine. We treasure still the hours
Made golden bright by common joy, and all
The dear companionship of daily life,—
Made up of little pleasures, cares, and hopes,
So sweet when shared, with tenderness alike,—
And live them o'er. And though unto mine eyes

It never has been given to pierce the veil
That hangs between this world and that wherein
She dwells, those wiser far than I — and true
Unto the truth, as stars unto the night,
Light to the morn, and buds unto the spring —
Do firmly say our dear ones walk beside
Us day by day with sight, e'en as with love;
And it may be, with vision clearer grown,
She sees more fully all my life's deep needs,
And with a tender love, e'en as of yore,
Gives to me still her faithful ministry,—
A guardian angel, as in Holy Writ.

And do not say, with thought to comfort me,
That the dear hands, which always busied were
In kindly offices, are folded now,
And all their work complete; for 't were a cross,
Indeed, to her whose whole unselfish life
Was effort gladly made for others' sake,
To idly live the long years through.   Whether

In this, or in some world beyond the sun,
Her joy must still in help to others be ;
Though know we not the work that waited her.

And say not, where mine ears may hear the words,
" She died ! "   There is no death !   When she went
    forth,
Her spirit, brave and strong, its outworn case
Of prisoning clay broke grandly through, and rose,
On wings of joy, unto that life wherein
No pain or grief or night can ever come.
It was her birthday in a happier world !

Joy and Pain.

One, of the poet's art,
Hath said, that in each heart
　Are chambers twain ;
And there two brothers dwell,—
Aye, dwell, and reign, as well,—
　Called Joy and Pain.

Alas ! hearts are today
Where Joy hath ne'er held sway,
　And Pain is king.
But, as our God is good,
By book and holy rood
　These words I sing :

One day, by waiting long,
Grown brave and calm and strong,
  As heir to throne,—
Who hath been, from his right,
Held by usurper's might,—
  Claiming his own,

Joy will triumphant reign
For aye, in place of Pain,
  For right must have its way;
And hearts, that long have bled,
With bliss at last are wed.
  God haste the day!

Invalided.

Thy pity, Lord, for those who lie
With folded hands and weary eye,
And watch their years go fruitless by,
    Yet know not why!

Who long, with spirit valiant still,
To work with earnest hand and will,—
Whose souls for action strive and thrill,
    Yet must be still!

Who smell in dreams the clover sweet,
And crush the wild fern 'neath their feet,
And seek each well-loved haunt and seat,—
    Each old retreat;

And mark again the birds' quick flight,
The river glancing in the light,
The blue hills melting from the sight,
    The starry night,

The fields aglow with sun and bloom,
The cloudless sky, the leafy gloom ;
Then wake to low and darkened room,
    Their world, a tomb!

Dear Lord, forgive ! if, as they lie,
And sadly watch their lives drift by,
Pain-torn, in anguish sore, they cry,
    "I would know why!"

Up or Down.

From a casement that oped on a narrow street,
   Where houses were dingy and poor and forlorn,
Two maidens looked forth the day to greet,
   And their faces were fair in the light of morn.

But one looked down on the ill-kept way,
   The miry pools, and the pavement rent,
That rarely were warmed by a single ray
   Of the beautiful sun the dear God sent;

At the tiny yards, where no grasses grew,
   And garments, ugly and cheap and worn,
Swaying in air that never knew
   How sweets in the heart of the rose are born;

At a pallid girl with a wailing child;
   A laborer, shabby and bent with toil;
And a youth whose eye was fierce and wild,
   Telling the tale of a soul's turmoil;

And an anguished cry from her heart arose,
   " 'T is a weary world, full of sadness and strife !
No love for us mortals the great God knows;
   No blessing is there in the gift of life ! "

The other looked up to the delicate blue,
   The lofty walls could not wholly hide,
And watched it deepen in warmth and hue,
   Till the banners of morning were floating wide.

A steeple tall she saw on the right, —
   The church where she learned a Father's care;
On the left a gold cross met her sight,
   And she thought: "They are kind to the orphans there."

From a roof near by some pigeons flew,
   And their soft tints shone in the morning light;
And the topmost branch of a tree, that grew
   In a neighboring street, she marked with delight.

As she watched it wave in the gentle air,
   Wondering if birdlings had no fear,
And if even then they were building there,
   A robin's matin thrilled her ear;

And she clasped her hands with a rapturous sigh,
   Crying, "Life is sweet, and the world is fair!
God watches us all with a loving eye,
   From children of earth to fowls of the air!"

Her First Sunday in Heaven.

Why do we pause and listen,
   Delay with unclosed door,
As though we fain would welcome,
   Within the fold, one more?

The music of childish footfalls
   Echoes along the aisle;
But we miss one step familiar,
   And the light of a sunny smile.

We scan the groups before us,
   Each fair and youthful face;
One little form is missing
   From its accustomed place.

The chorus of fresh young voices
   Swells on the waiting ear;
But her accents, sweet and girlish,
   We list in vain to hear.

And the tears from our eyes are falling,
   And to sing we strive in vain ;
The words we cannot utter,
   For our lips are dumb with pain.

But I think, when the children in Heaven
   Today make their anthems ring,
The angels will smile with pleasure,
   To hear a new voice sing.

So, though the tears unbidden
   To our lids will press and fall,
Let our hearts send up thanksgiving
   To Him who loveth all,

That while we weep and are lonely,
   This best day of all the seven,
To her it is one of gladness,
   Her very first Sunday in Heaven.

Come Back.

Oh mother, dear mother, come back to thy child,
If but for one moment, her grief is so wild!
Leave thy shining companions, the land of bright
    homes,
And come where in darkness a sad mortal roams.
I reach my arms toward thee! I listen, I pray:
From the city celestial, oh come, come away!

Oh come to me, mother! I long for thee so!
Let me look in thy face, with its bright, loving glow;
What rapture 't would be to see once again
Thy form in its freedom from weakness and pain;
And to hear the dear voice—ah, that were the best!—
That soothed me when lying a babe on thy breast!

Oh come but to tell me thy joy is complete,
That bright, fragrant blossoms spring up round thy
    feet;
That sweetest communion is held, day by day,
With the loved ones we tearfully saw pass away;
And lay thy dear hand, as of old, on my hair,
And steal from my heart all its sadness and care.

Then kiss me farewell, and return to the blest,
While thoughts of thy coming still gladden my
    breast;
And all through the years that I walk here alone,
The proof of thy gladness shall stifle each moan;
And the griefs of this life all as nothing will be,
While I journey, dear mother, toward Heaven and
    thee.

At the Tomb of Dickens.

I CANNOT turn me from this tomb,
   I 've crossed the seas to find,
And leave no sign, no leaf or flower,
   Of all my love behind.

Nor can I go ere I have laid,
   Above this sacred dust,
Some blossom sweet, to tell her love;
   It were to break a trust!

And so upon this hallowed spot,
   By which I reverent stand,
I cast this little wreath of verse,
   With fondly lingering hand.

And when the angel, fair and strong,
    Who nightly guards the dead,
Walks forth with soundless, weightless feet,
    'Neath his transforming tread,

May this poor garland, scentless now,
    And lifeless, like the tomb,
Change till it glows, when morning comes,
    A wreath of living bloom!

In Chains.

As the village clock, in its tall church-tower,
Tolls for the death of the midnight hour,
Through the shadows dark of the silent street,
With shrinking form, and with halting feet,
    Walks a man in chains,—

In galling chains, though no clanking sound
Awakens the echoes that sleep around;
Aye, and though never a link may gleam
In the silver moon's uncertain beam,
    They are riveted close.

And the fetters, that weigh on his form like lead,
Are dragging him down to a place with the dead,
Are crushing his brain and soul and heart;
For he's slave to a demon of cruel art,
    And a giant's strength.

With head bent low,—lest the night's pure eyes,
The stars that shine in the arching skies,
Should meet his own, and, meeting, betray
The grief of Heaven o'er his downward way,—
      He stumbles on.

Oh tender moon, draw over thy face
Yon floating veil of cloud-spun lace;
For never, in all thy nightly round,
Is a picture sadder, more terrible, found,
      Than that thou seest.

Oh star-eyed flowers, with night-dews bright,
Well may ye weep at this pitiful sight;
And, weeping, add to the numberless tears
Of the sorrowful women, whose prayers and fears
      Are for such as he.

Oh winds that are passing, well may ye sigh,
And join your wail to the human cry,
That, like a miserere grand,
Is rising all over our fair young land,
      From millions of hearts,

For him who was made in God's own shape,
Who has maddened his blood with the blood of the
　　　grape,
Who has sold his freedom, his self-command,
For the chain that binds him foot and hand,
　　　　In slavery.

Oh God, thou hast broken the African's chain;
Thou canst free from the bondage of sin and its
　　　pain!
With the might of thy love break the fetters, we
　　　pray,
That the man of weak will is wearing today,
　　　　Where'er he be found!

Give him courage to strive till his freedom's reborn!
Give him hope to look forward to victory's morn!
Give him strength for the task, from thine infinite
　　　store,
Of rising from serfdom to manhood once more,
　　　　Oh God, we implore!

The Burial of a Master.

Why is the mansion open?
 Why are its doors flung wide?
Has the master come to the country,
 In the dreary winter-tide?

Has he stolen a day from the city?
 Has he broken from toil and care,
While the snows lie deep on the meadows,
 And the woods are brown and bare?

Has he bidden his friends assemble?
 Do they come at his welcome call?
Will the music of happy voices
 Steal out through the ivied hall?

Then why is he not at the portal,
　With welcoming voice and hand?
And why do the loved ones enter,
　A hushed and awestruck band?

All silently through the portal,
　One guest unbidden passed.
Though no eye saw him enter,
　The shadow, which he cast,

Has turned the day into darkness,
　Has clouded our eyes with grief;
For his hand has bound the master,
　As the reaper binds the sheaf.

Was he mightier than the master,
　Whose giant brain had planned
The rending of the mountain,
　And the rushing river spanned? —

Who had made, far over the prairie,
  Where the golden poppies grow,
And out through the forest primeval,
  The ways where millions go? —

More potent than he whose magic
  The crystal wave of the lake
Had sent through hills of granite,
  The city's thirst to slake?

Aye, mightier than the master,
  As the gale beyond a breath,
As the torrent than a brooklet.
  Was 't the messenger of death?

Nay, not of death, my brother, —
  No soul was made to die, —
But of life, that is God our Father,
  Who calls to his work on high;

For the mind of great achievement,
    And noble activity,
Will soar unto heights far grander,
    From earth's limitations free;

A heart, in all life's changes,
    Tender and brave and true,
Through the ages, with each pulsation,
    Must its strength of love renew.

Over the hills and meadows,
    That lie in their shroud of snow,
The winter winds are chanting
    A requiem sad and low;

But within the trees' dry branches,
    And beneath that shroud of snow,
The buds are only waiting
    God's own good time to grow.

And down in hearts now deadened,
By the chilling winter of grief,
The germs of hope are still lying,
That shall burst into flower and leaf.

Departure of the Old Year.

THROUGH hope and fear, the dear Old Year
   Has walked beside me day by day.
He 's weary grown, and bent and gray;
   Tonight he goes away.

O'er river sealed and frozen field,
   O'er mountain high and meadow low,
White as his beard lies thick the snow,
   That he unheard may go.

Oh dear Old Year, 't is dark and drear!
   It storms without; why go so soon?
Wait for the rising of the moon,
   And grant, meanwhile, this boon.

Blot from your book, where every look
  And word and deed of mine are set,
Each thought and action I regret,
  Each unforgiven debt!

And, oh, I pray, take not away
  One joy into my life you've wrought;
But of the griefs that you have brought,
  Kind Year, oh leave me naught!

I wait his word. No sound is heard
  But sad-voiced bells! — Their dirge is o'er.
The dear Old Year will come no more;
  The New is at the door!

The Old and the New.
A Song of Progress.

Dim grow the shores of the Old,
    Fast do they fade from our view;
With hearts that are buoyant and bold,
    We steer for the realms of the New.

Then adieu to the land of the Old!
    All hail to the world of the New!
Farewell to the life that is told!
    Welcome the coming, the true!

Though by chains of outworn thought,—
    Whose links were welded strong
At the forge where selfishness wrought,—
    We were held to the Old too long;

Though the rocks of prejudice grim
    Frowned dark on either hand,
And superstition's whim
    Stretched wide its bars of sand;

We are launched on the sea at last,
    We are leaving the land of the Old;
By God's help, on its shores we have cast
    Our greed for power and gold.

In the waters we're sailing o'er,
    The thought of self shall be drowned;
Like a pearl, on the strand before,
    The love for mankind shall be found.

Though the plains our feet have crossed
    Are scarred with many a grave,
No sigh for the stolen and lost
    Shall sadden the song of the wave.

Though the hills may still be seen
    Where justice was crucified,
No tear for the pain that has been
    Shall fall in the billow we ride.

Though the memories, one and all,
    Of the false and the cruel and weak,
From our hearts shall swiftly fall,
    Where the nymphs play hide and seek;

The thoughts of the sweet and the dear,
    The tender, the brave, and the true,
We will bear in our breasts, while we steer
    From the land of the Old to the New.

God grant that the holy and strong,
    Now freed from mortality's chain,
May swift through the ether throng,
    To dwell with us once again,

With presence that soothes like balm,
　With guidance that ne'er shall fail;
And when sleeping winds becalm,
　May their white wings fan our sail.

Dim grow the shores of the Old,
　Fast do they fade from our view;
With hearts that are loving and bold,
　We steer for the realms of the New.

Then adieu to the land of the Old!
　All hail to the world of the New!
Farewell to the life that is told!
　Welcome the coming, the true!

Two Prayers.

So sad is life, I cry:
"Father, oh let me die,
  That pain be o'er."
Yet, born of that same sigh,
Swift-winged the prayer doth fly,
"Oh God, not yet to die!
  Of days give more!"

Despite all loss and pain,
Though sorrows o'er me rain,
  More time I ask,
That, ere I leave this life,
With grief and anguish rife,
I earn my peace by strife,—
  Complete my task.

Birthday Hymn.

As o'er my lengthening chain of years,
  One backward glance is cast tonight,
I see the past stand forth, revealed
  By memory's sweet though saddening light,—
Each day a link within the chain;
  Some gemmed with flowers, some dimmed by tears,
But all, grief-stained or bright with joy,
  The records bear of vanished years.

Oh may the links that time shall add,
  Though few, some deeds of love entwine;
May faith and patience lend their rays
  To make the chain more brightly shine;
And may it neither rust nor break
  Till, stretched from earth to heaven above,
'T is firmly held within the hand
  Of Him whose truest name is Love!

Hymn for Help.

Oh God, in thy strength, on our weakness look down,
Each holy endeavor with victory crown,—
Each struggle for freedom from doubt and from sin,
From the foes that are lurking without and within!

Give power to the arm that would shelter the weak,
And language to lips that fain comfort would speak!
Oh strengthen the hand that would raise the opprest,
And give speed to the feet that would do thy behest!

Of each pure aspiration, each lofty desire,
Oh grant thou fulfilment, and draw us up higher!
Our efforts, unaided, can nothing avail;
Then give us thy help, or we faint and we fail,

Lend a Hand.

Lend a hand, lend a hand, in the work for the world!
Place these words on your banner, ne'er let it be furled,
Till sin, pain, and wrong from their turrets are hurled.

Lend a hand! Do not think that because yours is small,
Or because from your fingers no riches may fall,
It was meant you should render no succor at all.

There are eyes that are weeping where none wipe the tear;
There are hearts that are breaking for tidings of cheer;
There are sinners who'd turn from their sins were you near;

There are lips that are burning where none hold
 the cup;
There are children who starve for a bit and a sup;
There are forms that are sinking, your hand might
 hold up.

Lend a hand, lend a hand! There is coming a
 day
When He who shall weigh us to each one will say:
"Did you help every brother you could on the
 way?"

Sunset Hymn.

Night's curtain, with its fringe of gold,
   Droops low o'er all the earth ;
No little flowers their leaves unfold,
   No bird-song finds its birth.

And while, like benediction sweet,
   The silence floats along,
I come, oh Father, to thy feet,
   And lift my heart in song.

And as I gaze where sinks the sun,
   Slow fading from my sight,
I think of him, thy holy one,
   Who filled the world with light.

The sun, of Christ an emblem fit,
    In sinking to his rest,
Leaves clouds, with rose and opal lit,
    Along the golden west.

So, Father, grant that, when I go,
    Within some heart remain
Of hope or love a warmer glow, —
    That life be not in vain.

Benediction.

Night holds the world in her embrace;
   Her shades are round us rolled;
So may the mantle of thy grace
   Our spirits closely fold.

Softly as fall the snows, that lend
   Our earth her robe of white,
May sweet and perfect peace descend
   Upon our hearts tonight!

INDEX OF TITLES.

Advice to a Despairing Lover 175
Andrea's Discovery 170
An Old Old-Fashioned Flower 179
Arbor-day Song 154
Aurora's Coming 37
Autumn's Coming 28

Bee, The 24
Benediction 252
Bessie's Riches 143
Birthday Hymn 246
Birthday Letter to Flossie 124
Breath, A 72
Burial of a Master 234
By the Brook 22

Call to the Crocuses 70
Carcassonne 192
Castle by the Sea 200
Child and the Aster 128
Children's Saint 97
Child-times 197
Chime for a September Wedding 184
Come Back 227
Coming Home at Night 85
Cradle in which John Quincy Adams was Rocked . . 93

Daisies and Succory 53
Departure of the Old Year 239
Dependence 62
Dickens's Tomb 229
Dream of Schooldays 78

Easter Lilies 205

Giving 114
Greeting with Bluebells 183

Helping Zeke 137
Her First Sunday in Heaven 225
Hold Fast the Bright Hours 69
How They Started for the Fair 135
Hymn for Help 247

If I were a Boy instead of a Girl 117
In Chains 231
In the Meadows in June 14
Invalided 220
Invocation to the Hills 43

Jealous Ghost 163
Joy and Pain 218
Joy Doubled 11

Kitty's Birthday Party 122

Lady Marie's Mishap	111
Land Where We all Have Been	90
Lend a Hand	248
Loch Katrine	65
May Party	146
Mayweed	57
Milkweed-down	29
Mountain Emigrant	189
Mugwump	161
My Little Milkmaid	133
November Greeting	181
Old and the New	241
On the Hills	39
Our Christmas	157
Ploughman and his Children	196
Prisoner of the Snow Fort	120
Quest, The	18
Regret	61
Santa Claus's Sister	103
She Is Not Dead	215
Spiranthes	31
Spring Pasture	26
Sunset Hymn	250
Sunset on the Bay	63

INDEX OF TITLES.

The Broader Field	207
To Woman Who Toileth	87
Two Prayers	245
Up or Down	222
Useless Little Tree	44
Usurer's Reply	173
Valentine Song	74
Wedding in the Garden	107
Welcome to Baby	186
When Pushed to the Wall	176
Where	12
Wild Gerardia	20
Woodbird's Song	209
Yellow-bird	55

INDEX OF FIRST LINES.

A child from the folds of his tiny gown 29
As o'er my lengthening chain of years 246
As the village clock in its tall church tower 231
Autumn's coming, even now 28

By the brook that laughs and plays 22

Coming in the glad midsummer 186
Could you but peep into this home 97

Daisies that faint in the noonday sun 53
Dear Flossie, I wish I might have something better . 124
Dim grow the shores of the old 241

From a casement that ope'd on a narrow street . . . 222

Give me of your strength and grandeur 43
Greenly grow, oh trees we've planted 154

Hast thou seen the lofty castle 200
Heigh 'o and heigh 'o! and o' heigh! 184
Herr Blumenthal, a Jew who dwelt 173
How sweetly as I dream advance 189

INDEX OF FIRST LINES.

I am naught but a little mayweed 57
I cannot turn me from this tomb 229
If you 're harrassed and hurried 176
I know of a land where we all have been 90
I'm sixty years, I'm growing old 192
In an earth-filled cleft of a rocky steep 44
I sing as sings the bird 11
It was cloudy at even, it stormed all night 120
I watched the cloudrack sweep the sky 24
I wish I owned a ship 135

Lady Rose and Sweet William were married 107
Lady Rose, Lady Rose 114
Lend a hand in the work for the world 248
Lover, sighing in despair 175

'Midst New Hampshire's hills of granite 137
Musing I glide o'er Katrine's Lake 65
My child, we were once little children 197

Namesake of the sweet cuckoo 18
Nay, tell me not, as one who knows not of 215
Night holds the world in her embrace 252
Night's curtain with its fringe of gold 250

Oh beautiful Aster, a little maid cried 128
Oh, do you know our Bessie 143
Oh fair is the morning 37
Oh God, in thy strength on weakness look down . . 247
Oh if I were a boy instead of a girl 117
Oh lady fair, thine ear incline 74

Oh let us not cling with vain sorrowing	69
Oh mother, dear mother, come back to thy child	227
Oh, oft in my dreams I am wandering still	26
Oh radiant lilies of glistening white	205
Oh the blue, blue sky is o'er me	14
Oh thou who sighest for a broader field	207
Oh where does the blush of the wildrose go	12
One of the poet's art	218
One winter's night a merry group	163
Our Kitty is five years old today	122
Over the ploughed ground, into the clover	111
Place a spray in thy belt or a rose on thy stand	87
Pray what do you see with your great brown eyes	39
So sad is life	245
The bluebird is calling, the spring rain is falling	70
There's a gay little yellow-bird flitting about	55
The wind's asleep, there's not a breath	63
This morn I flung open my casement	181
Though all the ornithologists	161
Though dark the night and the rough way long	85
Though grand and unending	62
Though the winds may roar	133
Through hope and fear, the dear old year	239
Through mazes bright of August bloom	20
Thy pity, Lord	220
To and fro, to and fro	93
Two lovers stood in the twilight dim	72

Weary and sad, one day	209
We did n't have much of a Christmas	157
Were I the summer breeze, dear girl	183
We sat and talked of storied days	170
We stood at a crowded counter	103
When the autumn days are here	31
When the god of sleep had touched me	78
Why do we pause and listen	225
Why is the mansion open	234
With gift of blossoms sweet and gay	179
With hearts as light as thistledown	146
Work with a will, work one and all	196
Wouldst dim this shining day	61

www.ingramcontent.com/pod-product-compliance
Lightning Source LLC
Chambersburg PA
CBHW032150230426
43672CB00011B/2505